A Drive Down the Coast

A DRIVE DOWN THE COAST

GETTING LOST ON THE BACK ROADS OF CALIFORNIA

RUSS DIBELLA

authorHOUSE®

AuthorHouse™
1663 Liberty Drive
Bloomington, IN 47403
www.authorhouse.com
Phone: 833-262-8899

Published by AuthorHouse 11/20/2020

ISBN: 978-1-6655-0635-9 (sc)
ISBN: 978-1-6655-0637-3 (hc)
ISBN: 978-1-6655-0636-6 (e)

Library of Congress Control Number: 2020921634

Print information available on the last page.

All interior photos taken by the author
Artwork concepts "Directional Signs" and "Snaking Road" by the author
Artwork concept "Snaking Road with Sunset" by Karl Moser
All artwork created by Karl Moser / Contact: karlmoserart@gmail.com

To My Father
For Encouraging the Journey and the Book

We do not take a trip; a trip takes us
~ John Steinbeck

ONE

The Road Less Traveled

Between the wish and the thing, the world lies waiting

~ Cormac McCarthy

Racing along the twisting, turning, tree-lined roads that gave way to open fields and farms brought the old, well-known proverb to life… the journey is indeed the reward. Full green canopies on the maple, birch and hickory trees lining the drive allowed only broken rays of early-morning sunlight to interrupt their shade helping to create long, leafy tunnels and a welcome feeling of solitude. A fragrant summer breeze combined easily with Sting's vocals and circulated throughout the cabin only adding to my contentment. And as I sang along in unison the miles rolled easily away.

Although speed wasn't essential, a seemingly inherent desire for it was always just beneath the surface and acting on that heightened my sense of awareness and delight. As the pace became quicker the turns felt sharper and the car began to rise and fall more easily over the straight and hilly runs. Where the path leveled off amid sprawling farms and wide open skies it took on an airy element of tranquility. Far-reaching views of the road ahead offered a comfortable measure of protection – however real or imagined – against the "powers that be" and the motor laws they enforced. Testing them was never far from thought; risk versus reward.

But soon enough the rustic charms of an old covered bridge or a large red barn would urge a downshift in both pace and adrenaline allowing me an opportunity to more easily and fully take in the surrounding scenery before reaching my eventual destination. To delight in the miles as much as possible before the drive was over – not unlike life itself.

Early mornings along the winding, scenic and relatively empty back roads and farmlands of eastern Pennsylvania and southern New Jersey always offered the best opportunity to own them. The anticipation of a good stretch of open road wending this way and that with few other cars in sight and time on my side was always reason enough to get moving sooner than later.

Getting there – it was all in a day's work.

I discovered early on in my former professional life that simply because there was a business meeting at the other end didn't mean I had to take the road more traveled to get there. Main roads and highways – or mileage disposal routes – undoubtedly served their purpose when absolutely necessary. But even under those circumstances I was rarely interested in the shortest distance between two points. Rather, I've always maintained that if work was to be done why not make it as enjoyable as possible?

Whether a leisurely drive to nowhere in particular, a backroad trek to the Jersey shore or an occasionally unwelcome slog to see a client across the Delaware River, I was inclined to follow my own interpretation – the most *scenic* distance between two points. Taking in picturesque surroundings, getting lost in the lyrics to songs and even making mental notes of roads that may be worth another pass at some other time often found me leaving the work to my arrival and remaining well and contentedly in the moments between. After all, as that other well-known proverb so rightly affirms, "All work and no play…"

Paying off in the form of lifelong memories and fulfilling new interests, a trip to San Jose, California soon after high school led to an impromptu southwest trek along Highway 17 sparking an early and unexpected attraction to scenic driving – and to California in general. With each passing road sign seemingly shouting out the potential perils of the road ahead – "Falling Rocks," "Road Narrows" and "Dangerous Curves Next Several Miles" – my concentration intensified; fluctuating between the visual and physical. This new and exciting experience, complete with friends, music and great weather, quickly resonated with me – even as a mere passenger. And as we sped along the winding and mountainous track toward the coastal town of Santa Cruz I recall being gripped by the newness of it; very much looking forward to the return trip… and to one day being in the driver's seat along this and other similar runs.

Little did I know at the time we were driving on what has long been considered one of California's most dangerous roads. With a series of sharp turns and blind curves, crashes on the nearly thirty-mile commuter stretch were frequent; recently hitting a ten-year high. But there's something about the mingling of magnificence and vulnerability that seems to attract. A dalliance between two dissimilar entities that make it one, offering a fuller return on investment than either individually. The excitement of spontaneity in our still-relatively formative years is beyond intriguing. And with little regard for much more than the here-and-now, that can lead to… complications. Psychology offers, in short, that our teenage brains aren't yet capable of comprehending the potential consequences of our actions and that risks, when the outcome is entirely unknown, aren't considered quite so risky. I would offer, much more simply, that ignorance is bliss… and not all bad.

But this appreciation for the landscape and back roads doesn't always require or even involve unpredictable circumstances. More often the grandeur is simply in and of itself, occasionally improved by comparisons – or perhaps confident memories. As was the case in San Jose when first seeing the abundant and lush foliage along miles of highway medians as they stood in stark contrast to the mostly featureless concrete dividers back home. Or the endless views of golden-brown and tan hills that seemed to encircle the city from every angle captivating me with their size and splendor. And, of course, the first truly tangible evidence of that iconic symbol of tropical climates and vacations – the sultry and swaying palm tree (only one species of which is native to the state – the California fan palm). Whether tall or short, palmate or pinnate, they were undeniable confirmation that I was "not in Kansas anymore."

If the grandeur can be enhanced somewhat by contrast and memory, then the driving experience – as with life in general – can be enriched considerably by way of music. An agreeable soundtrack can dictate the mood of the road as much as wheels, weather, traffic or terrain – adding to the exhilaration or relaxation in equal measure. It can evoke emotions and memories taking you on mental side trips to your past, present and even your future… all while you roll blissfully along.

In *Living with Music,* American writer Ralph Ellison wrote extensively about the influence of music and its role in our lives and cultures:

> "One of the chief values of living with music lies in its power to give us an orientation in time. In doing so, it gives significance to all those indefinable aspects of experience which nevertheless help to make us what we are. In the swift whirl of time, music is a constant,

reminding us of what we were and of that toward which we aspire. Art thou troubled? Music will not only calm, it will ennoble thee."

The enduring connection between music and driving dates back to the early 1930s when the first built-in radio, the Motorola, became a standard feature in cars after being successfully demonstrated in a Studebaker. The name was a combination of "motorized" and "Victrola" – the latter being the original phonograph player created in 1906 by the Victor Talking Machine Company in Camden, New Jersey. As automobile designs progressed over the next several decades, in-car audio equipment options kept pace – with improvements that continue to this day.

The image of a couple on the open road in a convertible in the 1950s complemented by the sound of AM radio and the early stages of rock'n'roll forever linked driving and music in the American psyche – particularly those of maturing adolescents. American writer Mike Edison comments on the upshot of this advancement in his book, *Sympathy for the Drummer - Why Charlie Watts Matters*:

> "In terms of teenage rebellion, putting radios in cars was just about the best thing that ever happened. The first wave of rock'n'rollers now had a mode of escape, and it came with a soundtrack *and* a backseat. You didn't have to be a soothsayer or advanced sociologist to see where that happy equation was headed."

In the ensuing years cars would have FM receivers, turntables (the "Highway Hi-Fi"), eight-track players, stereo sound, cassette decks and CD players well before Bluetooth technology and Internet service options began taking the reins in the 21st century. In that relatively short span of time, musical means went from being big, bulky and physical to small, smaller and virtual. And yet, despite its current state of near absence in the physical sense, it has never been more present in our culture.

As such, we've begun to take a much closer look at this connection to music – notably its wide-ranging but very real influence on our lives behind the wheel. Extensive driving studies have been conducted both here in the United States and abroad and the results seem to vary widely, suggesting everything from it being perfectly safe (even helpful) to being a major cause of accidents (even deadly). Study participants included a cross section of ages, genders and experience levels and the musical styles ranged from hard rock and soft rock to country, reggae, hip-hop, jazz and classical. In most cases drivers were allowed to choose the music for their respective drives as assigning anything potentially incompatible would most likely show inauthentic results. Additional criteria included volume levels, traffic, road conditions and other miscellaneous considerations.

Regardless of all these circumstances and methods by which data was observed and collected, there wasn't one predominant conclusion or interpretation – and in many cases findings among the studies seemed to be contradictory. However, one common thread among a handful of studies showed a correlation between safe driving and the beat of the music.

According to Psychologist Dr. Simon Moore of London Metropolitan University, participating drivers who listened to music which most closely mimicked the typical resting human heart rate – approximately sixty to eighty beats per minute – exhibited the safest driving habits. His belief is that music at this tempo doesn't affect a driver's adrenaline or mood to the extent that it becomes a factor in how they drive. Conversely, the ability to effectively control driving speed and reaction time proved more difficult while listening to music at higher tempos. And these control issues don't seem to be exclusive to the listener. In his book, *Traveling Music: The Soundtrack to my Life and Times,* Canadian drummer and writer Neil Peart (who passed away during this writing) wrote similarly how "one of the hardest challenges for a drummer, when your heart and adrenaline are racing, is to keep your *playing* from racing too."

Further, with historians and anthropologists having yet to discover a culture without music, it seems we may be prewired for this heart-beat and music-beat connection. In *The Power of Music: Pioneering Studies in the New Science of Song*, American music documentarian and author Elena Mannes writes that "science today is showing that music is in fact encoded in our bodies and brains... and that it has something to do with the evolution of our species." She reported on a study from the University of Cape Town, South Africa where a small hydrophone (waterproof microphone) was inserted into the uterus of a woman in the early stages of labor. One observation, called the startle response, found that when music was played the fetal heart rate became slightly elevated in response to the beat of the music. Other studies showed the heart rates mirroring those of their respective mothers when music heard by the mothers was deemed by them to be either stressful or soothing.

It seems obvious that music has the ability to transcend the merely audible and effect a far more visceral response in any number of situations. Which is very likely why musicians say they "feel" it quite literally when playing and why listeners say a song "moves" or "touches" them when heard. Indeed it can arouse countless emotions and physical responses. Suffice it to say... music is powerful. And the connection between music and driving, which has proven equally powerful for nearly a century, shows no signs of letting up. As long as there are cars, scenic roads and travelers to drive both so, too, will there will be music along for the ride.

One of many leafy South Jersey back roads

Just as an exceptional short story always seems to end too soon so, too, does a brief but enjoyable trip only leave me wanting more. And when a recent bout of this restlessness was finally met with opportunity, I decided to create an adventure of my own by stealing away on a leisurely and meandering solo drive along some of the most picturesque coastal back roads I could find. Those inviting to the traveler, but not so much the daily commuter. And in an effort to expand on those previous and often more time-restricted efforts throughout Virginia, Maryland, Delaware, Pennsylvania and Connecticut (even some in my own back yard of New Jersey), it would require new roads, new views and new horizons. As the appeal of California and that memorable drive along Highway 17 remained, a well-known line popularized by American journalist Horace Greeley came to mind offering some sage advice in the process (its true origin and authorship much debated): "Go west, young man, go west and grow up with the country."

What began as natural footpaths for early man to find food and water eventually morphed into a more advanced system of trade routes consistent with increasing populations and the advent of cities and towns. Communication and commerce as well as the eventual need for military transport were additional factors that led to the development of more sophisticated roadways around the world. The Egyptians, Carthaginians and not least the Romans (whose network of roads was considered the best engineered, finest built and most complex in their day) were all integral to this early evolution.

Later, 18th-century English engineers introduced technology to the process furthering construction efforts to include bridges, crested surfaces and less costly production methods. Opportunity for profit soon caught up with all these advancements and when private roads started being built – each summarily blocked by a pole (called a pike) – the toll road was created. While history offers various reasons for this, one of the most noted is monetary gain. When the required fee was paid by a traveler, the owner of the road would swing (or turn) the pole away allowing them access. The term "turnpike" was soon adopted in reference to the barriers. But by the mid-18th century it became a designation of the actual roads.

Although various circumstances caused an ebb and flow in roadwork development over the next several decades, progress eventually waned even more during the last half of the 19th century due to the building of canals and the continued growth of railroads. But when bicycle enthusiasts and manufacturers began to actively push for an improvement of the nation's roadways, steady progress began in earnest and the Good Roads Movement was established. This movement, which would coincide with and greatly benefit the emerging automobile industry, was essentially the catalyst for all future highway growth and expansion.

As a result, we now have a vast, extensive and well-maintained system of roads dotted with more than a few that are widely considered exceptional, both from scenic and driving perspectives. In *Deep South – Four Seasons on Back Roads*, American travel writer Paul Theroux wrote that "the long, improvisational road trip by car… in many respects a Zen experience… is quintessentially American." Add to any of these prospective back roads a soundtrack, either of preference or chance (ah, the randomness and spirit of radio), and you have the makings of an outstanding asphalt excursion.

From the diverse and rolling landscape of meadows, farms and mountains along the Blue Ridge Parkway (Virginia to North Carolina) lyrically celebrated in John Denver's "Take Me Home, Country Roads," to the primarily flat terrain of the historic Route 66 (Chicago to Los Angeles) immortalized as the "Mother Road" in John Steinbeck's *The Grapes of Wrath,* nearly every part of the United States has at least some roads well worth traveling.

And the less traveled the better.

TWO

Off On Your Way

Wherever I have wandered, a path has appeared

~ Alice Walker

After an all-day, cross-country trek, I walked out of the Rogue Valley International airport into the somewhat unexpected heat of Medford, Oregon – this starting point strategically chosen to minimize air travel and avoid any backtracking or repetition along my drive (which would "officially" begin in California). Although early August, it was my understanding that the northwest was seasonally cooler than other parts of the country. But with an almost exclusive fondness for summer conditions and knowing I needed good weather in my favor, I welcomed the clear skies and heat as a positive omen. My belief was that it would only enhance the overall experience – especially considering this was rescheduled from the previous February when unusually heavy rains caused coastal flooding, landslides and impassable road conditions along many sections of my loosely planned route. Even though my friend, Alex, offered insight that this may make for "more interesting driving and a better story," I erred on the side of caution understanding that this particular coastline, parts of which are precarious enough under *normal* circumstances, was likely to have proven far less enjoyable – if even possible – at the time. To his point, however, in *Deep South* Theroux also commented on the literary potential of these threatening forecasts and "more interesting" driving conditions:

> "This sort of dire warning... suggests to the wanderer a promise that by morning there will be something important and timely to chronicle. Bad news for the civilian is often welcome to the travel writer looking for a tale to tell. Wild weather sounded dramatic, and the worst weather had the effect of tormenting a landscape and putting it in sharp relief, giving it a face and a mood."

Though somewhat mapped out during the previous several months (a few sites to see, some planned roads to retrace, an anticipated visit, etc.), in essence it was done in pencil leaving room for quiet speculation about whether the reality would live up to my efforts... or amount to only a vague representation of them. Whether "the best laid schemes o' mice an' men" indeed would go awry (as they likely would have in February). But beyond that I didn't give it much thought – my mostly open-ended itinerary lending itself to that claim. I was looking for some true and relaxed travel – not just some brief version of removal with time constraints. It was "time to trust the magic of beginnings," as German philosopher Eckhart von Hochheim once said. But for fiscally responsible reasons I had to firm up one thing (at least on paper) – a date for a return flight. In so doing, and with no idea when I would actually be returning,

I allowed myself two weeks to explore the westernmost back roads of the California coast – from the Oregon border to the Mexican border – all in an effort to take this scenic driving thing to the next level. But that return flight was the only backend reservation I made knowing full well that it didn't matter much whether I kept it.

Eagerly hopping into my gunmetal gray rented Jeep and getting a hurried feel for the unfamiliar dashboard, I quickly landed the dial on a good, up-tempo driving song ("Without You" by the Doobie Brothers) and soon found my way to the most appealing route out of town to begin my journey south… by heading north.

The Redwood Highway spans approximately 285 miles from southeast of Grants Pass, Oregon to Leggett, California. And even though it has a few numerical state-route designations, this is the segment of the highway as it pertains to driving among the "big trees" and renowned scenery – including several national and state parks as well as beaches, nature trails and myriad other recreational and visual enticements. Although the true redwood experience had to first be earned by way of several miles of four-lane driving both north and east along the Pacific Highway (not to be confused with California's Pacific Coast Highway), as I passed the towns of Central Point, Gold Hill and Rogue River the changing scenery became increasingly apparent. A parallel run with the Rogue River near Gold Hill Bridge further suggested that towns would soon be falling away in favor of some serious wilderness. And after winding my way through the (Josephine) county seat of Grants Pass and the community of Selma near the base of Eight Dollar Mountain – so named for the value of a gold piece once discovered there – a recurrent stretch of small and wooded settlements eventually found me within striking distance of the Oregon-California border.

One of the smallest towns I passed had the appealing name of Wonder reminding me of a quote by Socrates that's been locked in memory since college: "For wonder is the feeling of a philosopher, and philosophy begins in wonder." *Psychology Today* describes wonder as "a complex emotion involving elements of surprise, curiosity, contemplation and joy... brought about by a marvel ('wonderful thing')" – the very elements that inspired this road trip and which resulted in the many "wonderful things" discovered along the way. Fittingly, I wondered about the origin of the name and quickly scribbled it in my journal for some end-of-day homework – how I began referring to my daily post-drive writing and research. This downtime allowed me to describe the day's events and sightings in greater detail offering a better chance at effectively pursuing what was then my next, as yet undefined writing project. American writer John Steinbeck wrote similarly (if not to some extent dispiritedly) about the importance of making time to gather thoughts while on the road in his 1962 book *Travels with Charley - In Search of America*:

> "I had parked well away from the road and from any traffic
> for my time of rest and recount. I am serious about this.
> I did not put aside my sloth for the sake of a few amusing
> anecdotes. I came with the wish to learn what America is
> like. And I wasn't sure I was learning anything."

It turns out the name Wonder simply stuck when, in 1902, residents of the nearest town a few miles north began wondering how the owner of a newly opened general store in an area with hardly any locals (fewer than twenty-five at the time) would draw any customers. But when "Wonder Store," as the owner came to call it, began serving a growing number of residents, one by one the newly built post office, rail station and small private airport each took the name; effectively helping to land Wonder on the map.

Nearly thirty miles south of Wonder I began to get a feel for some of the driving I came to experience as the dense foliage of the Siskiyou Mountains closed in around me. Although not the highest subrange in the Klamath Mountains, its proximity to the Pacific Ocean creates ample rainfall resulting in some of the heaviest vegetation in the area. The upshot of this is a beautiful mix of lush green groundcover out from which rise tall oaks and firs; collectively lessening the effects of the midday sun. Quietly thanked and invited to "Come Back Soon" by way of a small and modest road sign just north of the border, my brief but enjoyable drive through southwest Oregon was quickly ending. But I was soon being warmly greeted by yet another sign – this one much larger, more colorful and proudly displaying an equally impressive depiction of its state flower.

"Welcome to California" shone brightly against an ocean-blue background and alongside the matching golden blooms of a California poppy; officially deemed a fitting symbol for The Golden State in 1903 (even though this nickname wasn't adopted for another sixty-five years). The sign alone evoked an optimism befitting its Greek state motto: "Eureka!" – its English translation doubling for me as a suitable rallying cry that would apply many times on this journey: "I have found it!" Soon after crossing the border into our 31st state and into its northwestern-most county, Del Norte ("of the north"), the road vanished into the woods where the anticipated became reality and the feeling – as well as the driving – intensified.

The "official" start of my drive

American writer Bill Bryson wrote powerfully (and often humorously) about world travel and described the enormity and power of the woods in *A Walk in the Woods - Rediscovering America on the Appalachian Trail:*

> "Woods are not like other spaces… their trees surround you, loom over you, press in from all sides. Woods choke off views and leave you muddled and without bearings. They make you feel small and confused and vulnerable. Stand in a desert or prairie and you know you are in a big space. Stand in a woods and you only sense it. They are a vast, featureless nowhere. And they are alive."

The Siskiyou Mountains immediately proved an impressive starting point and I was fortunate that my travel plan allowed for nearly all one-hundred miles of the sweeping southwest arc to be followed – from Medford, Oregon to Crescent City, California. Although the backdrop of mountain peaks, redwoods and imposing rocky passes whetted my visual appetite, being flanked by such considerable land formations for that duration in an unfamiliar territory was initially somewhat intimidating. As Bryson noted, everything indeed seemed to "press in from all sides" and I began to wonder about the scenic aspect of it. Was I too close to my surroundings to have perspective? Would the actual driving require too much attention? Will I quite literally not see the forest for the trees?

I was reminded of a similar unfamiliarity and mild apprehension that accompanied a drive taken twenty-six years earlier in Quintana Roo, Mexico with my wife Kelley. In lieu of a bus trip where we'd be at the mercy of a set schedule, we decided to rent a Jeep and drive from our hotel in Cancun to the Mayan ruins of Xel-Há ("spring water") and Tulum ("wall"). Even though it was a fairly straight coastal run, the mostly deserted, scenic two-lane was situated slightly inland passing through nearly eighty miles of dense foliage. With few stops or structures along the way – most of those only nondescript, thatched-roof huts or empty lots where homes or shops once stood; the footprints and remnants of their uncertain foundations still evident – it seemed at once both bleak and beautiful. But any concerns we had about safety or a lack of scenery were soon replaced with a sense of adventure and appreciation as we remained enjoyably in the moment throughout our intrepid little daytrip.

One somewhat-poignant memory, captured on my then-ever-present video camera and which spoke to a culture and time before this part of Mexico became even more the major tourist destination it is today, was stopping at the lone gas station – little more than a modest structure with a single gas pump situated on a dirt lot essentially in the middle of nowhere. After pulling in to fill up on our return to Cancun, I was taken aback by the attendant's youth. And in my rather limited and fragmented Spanish I asked, "Cómo te llamas – quantos años?"

"Juan – siete," he replied.

In spite of the fact that he seemed as adept as any adult, both at his job and in speaking with customers, it gave me pause to think a seven-year-old was pumping gas instead of going to school or playing with friends. And as

I paid him in pesos, the more apt and welcome smile of a little boy crossed his face and he offered a quiet "gracias" before turning away.

Fewer than three miles south of the Oregon border around a soft blind curve a sharply contrasting concrete and stone façade two lanes wide and more than thirty feet high quickly came into view. Bordered by trees right up to and over its well-lit entrance, the Randolph Collier Tunnel – named for the "Father of the California Freeways" – cut into the side of Oregon Mountain offering travelers a shortcut of less than half a mile to the opposite side. As I continued on, it dawned on me in a whimsical sort of way that for those few brief moments I was literally driving *through* part of California. Later that evening during homework time I discovered that prior to 1963 this crossing was only possible by way of a slow and meandering, over-mountain pass called Oregon Mountain Road (originally a wagon route in the late 1850s). I recalled seeing that name on a street sign by a turnoff about a mile prior to the tunnel, but thought nothing of it other than being satisfied with finally knowing, in a general sense, where I was. With its 128 turns, multiple switchbacks and gravel summit, it sounded far more appealing to me than a straight and simple run through a tunnel. By its very design and purpose another version of the shortest distance between two points. And had I known about it as I planned my trip in the months prior, that road that Collier once called "an old Jeep path" would have been exactly that once again.

I would have preferred the 1850 wagon route

Several miles and a handful of songs later the unmistakable voice of the late Glen Frey filled the air with the opening lines of "Take it Easy." And as I, too, was "running down the road tryin' to loosen my load" I felt an immediate piecing together of my journey as the Eagles unsurprisingly became part of the evolving soundtrack. Although they came to symbolize the classic Southern California rock sound of the 1970s, unlike The Beach Boys a decade earlier none of the original Eagles were native Californians. But their 1971 formation in Los Angeles and the success of their debut album a year later solidified their connection to the Golden State – just as reflections of many visits have reinforced my (and countless others') fondness for it.

In his biography, *CSNY: Crosby, Stills, Nash & Young*, English music journalist and author Peter Doggett describes in detail our early, comprehensive and continued attraction to California and the West Coast:

> "Successive waves of mythology – the gold rush, escape from the Dust Bowl, the fantasy factories of Hollywood – had swept millions of Americans west since the mid-nineteenth century, in search of the sun-blessed Shangri-la of California. In 1962... Life magazine devoted

an entire issue to 'The Call of California.' The photogenic potential of the West Coast made it an ideal subject for a pictorial journal. Those with more cultural yearnings might be enticed by the ripe jazz scene of San Francisco… and the Beat culture, as poets, musicians, and hipsters combined in passionate, transgressive adventures. The West Coast was easily sold as a beacon of hedonism… as the land of surf, sun, and endless beach parties."

As I continued along the Redwood Highway the lyrics seemed to answer some of those earlier questions about perspective and reminded me of my own plan to take it easy. To remain in the moment, observe my surroundings and allow the present to hold its charms. And even, somewhat atypically, to avoid any urge to pass slower vehicles on two-lane roads – no matter how frustrating that may become. It was, after all, an exploration of sorts. An opportunity to develop a comfortable rhythm with the road. Slow and steady would indeed win the race – as long as it wasn't *too* slow or *too* steady. As Frey so appropriately warned… *"Don't let the sound of your own wheels drive you crazy."*

My southwest trek continued throughout the bright August afternoon and became more stimulating as the mountain course began a steady descent toward the coast. With gravity sneaking up gradually signs warned to "Watch Your Downhill Speed" while others posted relatively sluggish speed limits. Both proved to be more than just good suggestions as the turns sharpened and the winding downward drive continued for the next forty miles. An elevation of nearly 1000 feet northeast of Patrick Creek dropped to sea level at Smith River and evidence of the major excavation work that went into creating this path was visible just outside my passenger door. Intimidating masses of exposed earth, stone and trees towered overhead and seemed to encroach upon the southbound lane while unassuming guardrails kept the northbound traffic from the ravine and river below. Only one lane apart – yet entirely different driving concerns.

The Smith River, named for 19th-century explorer Jedediah Smith, runs parallel to the highway from Gasquet (*Gas*-kee) to Smith River on its way to the Pacific Ocean. The only river in California that flows freely and naturally for its entire twenty-five miles, it's also part of one of the largest single and undammed river systems in the United States. Even though continuing west on the Redwood Highway would have taken me on what my GPS showed as a wonderfully meandering drive through Jedediah Smith Redwood State Park, following the river would offer a unique and simultaneous view of densely wooded mountains to my right and clear waters to my left. Accordingly, and with Smith River as my initial waypoint destination, I opted off the highway just east of the river to take this more scenic northwest route to its end at Highway 101.

As the river continued flowing diagonally to the coast, "The 101," as locals refer to it, took me north through the painterly backdrop of well-groomed, ocean-side farms extending into Smith River. At the northernmost end of town, set among the magnificent redwoods on the ancient tribal lands of the Native American Tolowa people lay the California-Oregon border. This part of the state, south to Wilson Creek, is where the Tolowa existed relatively unaffected by any outside influence until around 1850 (with the exception of an 1828 meeting with Smith and his exploring party). During the next decade the Tolowa population was reduced by more than half as a result of disease and deadly encounters with non-natives – an issue in American history that smolders to present day in the form of mixed opinion and debate. Due to their historical significance in this area, the Tolowa people are commemorated by way of several Park Commission and Historical Society plaques found on various northwestern California landmarks.

Noticeably cooler than inland, this part of the Wild Rivers Coast

(Bandon, Oregon to Orick, California) was to be my true point of departure. As such, I considered calling it a day and spending the night. The Howonquet Lodge at the ocean's edge along the Oregon border was imaginatively inviting and I immediately pulled into the parking lot more than ready to make camp. Built in tribute to the heritage of the Tolowa Tribe, it was beautifully appointed in an outdoorsy Native American motif – the large entrance portico very log cabin-esque – and I looked forward to exploring the grounds a bit more once settled. But the unwelcome news about a lack of available lodging (the last room had been assigned to the older couple in front of me) had me reluctantly but necessarily pressing on. As I would discover more than a few times on this trip, summer months along the California coast offer little in the way of unfilled hotel or motel rooms – no matter their unfavorable online ratings or lack of "character." As a result, for better or worse, my plan to wing it already appeared to be in full swing.

With sunset not too far off and that apparent shortage of hotel rooms, I pulled out my Rand McNally paper map and quickly scanned it for options. Setting a course south to the pleasant-sounding county seat of Crescent City, my hopeful expectation was that some vacancy signs would be awaiting me there. Just over the Smith River Bridge at Lake Earl Drive two very different types of "State" signs appeared, both pointing me in the same direction – but to very dissimilar places. Struck by this contrast – "Tolowa Dunes State Park" and "Pelican Bay State Prison" – I was nudged somewhat from the moment thinking about the disparity of a prison (actually a 275-acre, super-maximum security prison for the most violent offenders) situated in such a peaceful setting among farmlands, forests and mountains; the blue waters of the Pacific ("peacemaking") lapping at the shores of Pelican Bay only two miles to the west. And as farms slowly gave way to woods and I passed the prison entrance on my left, I couldn't help but be stirred by the freedom I had and was actively pursuing right outside those unforgiving walls. Only a short time earlier I was driving along a river that was flowing just as freely down the very mountains which serve as a backdrop to the prison – another sharp contrast that was hard to miss.

To be sure, the freedom of the open road is a much-celebrated and enjoyable one – indeed the primary focus of my journey. Needless to say, this was something which was not lost on me... least of all at that moment.

Crescent City, a small harbor town named for a crescent-shaped stretch of sandy beach south of the city, proved a fine place to end my day. With quaint and comfortable accommodations overlooking the harbor and situated on part of the Tolowa Indian Settlements, the forced continuation of my trip south from the comparatively modest Smith River was a definite improvement in setting. Views of the newly rebuilt Crescent Harbor Marina, the red-roofed Battery Point Lighthouse (seen in Tim McGraw's video for "Not a Moment too Soon") and even the fourteen-acre Castle Island Preserve just to the north and half a mile off the coast all added to the day's discoveries. But at this hour it was a variety of restaurants next to and across from the harbor that quickly caught my attention.

After checking in to my room and cleaning up a bit (to include a splash of cold water on my travel-weary face), I grabbed my journal and strolled along the waterfront to view the ocean and peruse the eateries; all pleasantly within walking distance of one another. Calm waters and clear skies along this northernmost harbor in California made for an easy and fitting end to all the day's scenery and one restaurant lured me in just as easily with a sign touting "Craft Beers & American Comfort Food" – the latter being the true draw.

The Northwoods Public House (origin of the term "pub") was busier than expected on that Tuesday night and I waited in the small lobby for a table while Heart's "Crazy on You" played in the adjacent bar. I had become accustomed to hearing them that day as their songs seemed to be in heavy rotation during much of my drive (as was the music of the Steve Miller Band a few days later while in the Bay Area). I attributed this increased airplay to the band hailing from the Pacific Northwest – specifically Washington and Vancouver, British Columbia. Although I was hardly in their hometown, musicians tend to be given favorable attention in and around their places of origin. So it was no surprise to hear them once again as I walked in and took a window seat across from the beautifully finished and well-stocked bar.

With some consideration to this appealing little harbor town and by now over the strains of "Somebody" by Bryan Adams, I ordered a drink and a seafood dish off the menu. And as my very pleasant server Jamie turned to leave, I settled back in my chair for a few moments of relaxed reflection – thankful for a day well spent. While looking around at the varied clientele of families, friends and co-workers – the latter of whom appeared so by their matching "uniform" of worn work boots, jeans and fluorescent vests – I briefly wondered about each of their stories. Then I reached for my journal, opened it and continued writing mine.

THREE

Hit the Open Road

Afoot and lighthearted I take to the open road

~ Walt Whitman

On a chilly harbor morning, the horizon misty yet the sky directly overhead bright with possibility, I set my sights on the first seaside drive of the trip. Even though a sufficient amount jet lag had the usual influence and woke me well before sunrise, I didn't hit the road until a short time later after some daybreak journaling and a leisurely (albeit modest) breakfast off the lobby. But if the time-zone change hadn't awakened me, the sporadic sound of the Crescent City Harbor fog horn would have done the trick soon enough. Situated atop a forty-foot-tall tower at the end of a jetty where the harbor meets the Pacific, it announces the presence of the rocky shoreline without discretion. Mariners, residents and tourists alike are all well within earshot in this very small town and, as such, are captive to its bellow – need it or not. In this telling, I'm reminded of Van Morrison's beautifully mellow "Into the Mystic" – *"When that fog horn blows, you know I will be coming home..."* – that metaphorical fog horn announcing the *end* of his travels; this very real one effectively marking the *start* of mine.

Stopping to take in that first view of the Northern California coast

Even though sonar, GPS and seabed-mapping technologies have rendered fog horns as more symbolic of the hazier fringes of maritime life, they apparently still retain their rightful role as navigational instruments in the nautical world. Stopping into the harbor office to ask a few questions, I was referred to the very pleasant and knowledgeable Crescent City Harbor Master Charlie Helms. Although he noted that the threat of technological advances was indeed relegating fog horns to the historical side of time, he quickly added that "audible ATON, or Aids to Navigation, systems are still used here and in many other places in poor- or low-visibility conditions like fog, rainstorms and even tsunamis… which Crescent City is known for."

That last one resonated with me as I had never before seen signs warning of a "Tsunami Hazard Zone" until heading to Crescent City. The only signs with a similar message that I recall seeing along the South Jersey shore indicated: "Coastal Evacuation Route" – which are posted primarily for hurricanes along the eastern and southeastern seaboard.

With none of those low-visibility conditions present (thankfully), I simply chose to view this predawn wail as the starting gun of my day and soon hopped on a promising coastal run down the Redwood Highway leaving the harbor in my rearview mirror. This initial trek along the northern California shoreline was more than welcome – though short lived. When the road turned inland and the blue of the ocean gradually vanished from view, another winding and mountainous stretch of deep greenery and towering redwoods took over. By design much of my journey was a relatively unbroken state of visual incentive; a mix of woods and water (as well as some musical and literary interludes) to hold my gaze and keep me present. In *Travels with Charley*, Steinbeck wrote about this considered approach:

> "From the beginning of my journey, I had avoided the great high-speed slashes of concrete and tar called 'thruways,' or 'super-highways.' These great roads are wonderful for moving goods but not for inspection of a countryside. And this is why, on my journey which was designed for observation, I stayed as much as possible on secondary roads where there was much to see and hear and smell, and avoided the great wide traffic slashes which promote the self by fostering daydreams."

The Del Norte Coast Redwoods State Park, deeply shaded with an array of beautifully winding mountain roads, was both a "Daylight Headlight Zone" and a "Scenic Route," as loosely designated by two roadside signs. I certainly understood both and could justify the first as somewhat necessary given the park's slightly reduced visibility and its travel both by unfamiliar tourists (guilty) and the many imposing logging trucks passing through – each weighing upwards of 80,000 pounds (one reason for the sporadic runaway-vehicle ramps). But based on all the consistent landscape beauty I had observed up to that point, the most recent example being stunning panoramic views of the Pacific from high atop various vista-point bluffs, my immediate thought about the second sign was, *"Haven't these all been scenic routes?"*

But soon after crossing Wilson Creek Bridge where the ocean lapped gently at the rocky shoreline of False Klamath Cove, a bend in the road brought me to the first tourist "attraction" of my drive... The Trees of Mystery. Though I could certainly appreciate the outward connection to nature and the likely educational value of it, the nearly fifty-foot-tall Paul Bunyan and commensurately smaller Babe the Blue Ox from American folklore – both beckoning passersby from outside a large museum and gift shop – told me it was precisely the type of kitschy "scenery" I had no interest in seeing. And after a brief stop (however ironically) to use the facilities, I was quick to escape the crowds and get back on the road.

Heading south toward Klamath along its namesake river, I encountered a pair of large concrete grizzly bears at the abutment to the Klamath River Bridge and immediately became curious about their bright gold appearance – standing in such stark contrast to everything else. They reminded me of an article I had previously read about two solid marble Chinese guardian lions (or "foo dogs") that sit mysteriously alone in the Mojave Desert along Route 66 in Amboy, California. These types of seemingly inconsequential observations always stayed with me and my curiosity was evident in a journal entry that simply asked: "Gold bears in Klamath?" That said, as the story goes...

The two California grizzly bears – the official state animal – still stand watch at the southwest entrance to a bridge no longer there. They have been reliably on the job at the site of the Douglas Memorial Bridge since its dedication ceremony in May of 1926. After the "Christmas Flood of 1964" took the bridge along with many Pacific Northwest towns, the bears – and the entrance – were all that remained. But unmistakably it was their storied history prior to the flood that earned them the right to endure.

Sometime in the late 1950s, as part of an effort to spruce up the small and tired town of Klamath, a group of local residents decided to surreptitiously paint the four original concrete bears gold – well before California's official designation as The Golden State in 1968. Although the people of the town didn't seem to mind, government officials apparently felt otherwise and – as this "tradition" continued for more than a decade – ordered highway workers to strip the paint after each infraction. But the rather persistent message of the locals eventually became clear – they liked their grizzlies gold – and the color was officially sanctioned upon completion of the new bridge just upriver in 1965. Today four "descendants" of the original bears sit atop the northbound and southbound guardrails on both sides of the Klamath River Bridge brightly welcoming and likely intriguing travelers from either direction.

After seeing these unique adornments and feeling inspired to learn their history, taking snapshots of bridges on this trip and later reading about them became somewhat of a practice for me. An opportunity to capture moments of progress on this vast nature "hike." Of moving forward to another place... always to somewhere else. As American essayist, philosopher and poet Ralph Waldo Emerson wrote in *Nature*; one of his posthumously published essays:

> "To the body and mind which have been cramped by noxious work or company, nature is medicinal and restores their tone. The health of the eye seems to demand a horizon. We are never tired, so long as we can see far enough."

Just north of the Humboldt County line I was enticed once again by that "S" word on a sign indicating a turnoff for the "Newton B. Drury Scenic Parkway." Named for the one-time director of the National Park Service and the Save the Redwoods League, it was an homage to a man whose efforts were integral to the creation of a national park system in California. Opting off the Redwood Highway for the more intimate confines of this two-lane path through Prairie Creek Redwoods State Park became immediately rewarding. Stopping for a brief hike to see the "Big Tree" (the 15th largest single-stem coast redwood at 286 feet tall and more than 1500 years old) was a bonus. The brief adjustment from twists and turns to this much straighter but far more shaded and secluded detour through towering old-growth redwoods, firs and spruce trees was a worthy tradeoff and I savored the miles of easy solitude.

The sign and emblems of nearly 132,000 acres of California woodland

A rustic split-rail fence at the southernmost end of the parkway fronted what I later learned was an expanse of golden wild oat, foxtail and filaree grasses extending from the road to the redwoods. This otherwise unassuming field abutting a stand of conifers was actually part of the Madison Grant Forest and Elk Refuge – a 1600-acre habitat for California's last surviving herd of Roosevelt elk. Although they've reportedly been increasing in number since my visit, an information sign at the site read like a detective story in search of the elusive beast: "On the Trail of the Elk - Every Move Leaves a Clue." As luck would have it, there were no clues and no elk on this day (I later discovered that sightings are more likely to occur during winter when the elk move to lower elevations in search of food and to avoid winter storms). Regardless, it was a fine way to round out the relaxing parkway drive before its final curve returned me once again to the Redwood Highway.

Heading southwest across Redwood Creek (it seems a lot of naming liberties are taken with those old redwoods... or "sequoia sempervirens"), I continued on and out to the coast where the river empties into the ocean at the former timber and mill town of Orick ("mouth of the river"). An evaporation fog lay low and patchy across Freshwater Lagoon to the east; an indication that the water was warmer than the midday air – still cool at only sixty-eight degrees. This serpentine track continued past the eastern rims of Stone Lagoon and Big Lagoon then rolled off toward the coast into the densely forested Patrick's Point State Park where spruce, red alder and pine trees outnumber the redwoods. Its unique ocean headland was beautifully adorned by meadows of wildflowers, to include a swath of vibrant rhododendrons.

A couple of surface roads followed the rugged and rocky coastline of sheer cliffs against the Pacific eventually taking me directly to the south-facing Trinidad Head Memorial Lighthouse. This "accurate replica" of the original 1871 structure sits right on the harbor in this small and sheltered seaside town of Trinidad. With clear skies and much warmer temperatures than earlier in the day, I decided it was the perfect time (and place) to take a breather and grab a bite to eat at the nearby and aptly named Lighthouse Grill.

The sound of "Let Her Cry" was playing overhead as I walked in and it evoked its usual pleasant memory for me; surely revealing an unwitting grin. As with all songs from their 1994 debut album *Cracked Rear View*, South Carolina's Hootie & the Blowfish always made me think of my twin daughters Alea and Kelsey as they were born that same year. One of the most successful albums of all time, it was played repeatedly on the radio for nearly two years and became the top selling album of 1995. And although the message in "Let Her Cry" isn't exactly cheerful, memories from those years are prized and, as such, hearing it brought to mind a welcome feeling of home.

Despite the music playing inside where I placed my order at the islandy walk-up counter, I took a seat at an outdoor table content to be off the road for the moment and sitting in the warmth of the sun. A fragrant sea breeze drifted through carrying with it the cry of seagulls and I wondered if either scent or sound was as noticeable to the locals as both were to this outsider. After making a few journal notes (one about their soft drinks being served in Mason jars: "A nice touch of originality..."), I opened my Kindle to read while waiting; always preferring to spend time rather than merely kill it. A mild distinction perhaps – but one with a one a reward.

The relative silence on the patio was soon broken by the very familiar sound of conga drums in the distance. Even more interesting to me was that there was no accompanying music – just a steady cadence of bass hits and open tones with high-end fills here and there (similar to their initial use during religious ceremonies, as instruments of war and even as a means of communication by cultures in many forested regions). While reading about the history of drums and percussion years ago, I learned that the term "conga" is actually of Latin American origin. And in Cuba it's typically applied only to the *rhythms* played during Carnaval – their local version of Mardi Gras. Cuban-born singer Gloria Estefan very clearly notes the conga as such – *"It's the rhythm of the island..."* – in Miami Sound Machine's 1985 song of the same name ("Conga"). In Cuba and most other Spanish-speaking countries the actual *drum* is more accurately referred to as a tumbadora (which has its origins in Rumba – the first music to use them specifically). Suddenly curious about this sound and drawn to discovering its source, I spent a few minutes walking the restaurant grounds looking and listening for it to no avail. All the same the mysterious yet melodious timbre; still sounding when my server came, was a pleasant, welcome and suitable addition to my afternoon stopover.

Immediately adjacent to the restaurant was the entrance to my next planned route... Trinidad to Moonstone Beach by way of Scenic Drive. The names alone were all encouraging enough. But the twisting, wooded and rocky shoreline drive appeared even more promising – both on my map and my GPS – and it had me eager to get back on the road. While fueling up across from the restaurant a customer at the next pump began making some small talk with me. Perhaps in his late-twenties with long hair and arms full of tattoos, he noticed my license plates and asked if I was from Washington State.

"No," I replied. "But I live only about 3000 miles east of there."

Laughing politely he said that he and his girlfriend are locals from Trinidad. That they see a lot of different license plates pass through and "it always makes us curious about where everyone's from."

"Well," I said, "I'm from New Jersey just down from Oregon in a rental from Washington and driving through California... for whatever that's worth."

After adding that my immediate plan was to head to Moonstone Beach, he almost apologetically advised that Scenic Drive was closed about a mile down coast and all traffic was being rerouted back to the entrance. Immediately thinking about my options, I simply thanked him for the information as he wished me luck and turned to leave. When I finished fueling up I thought about this simple exchange. Although I didn't know it yet, I would discover more than once on this journey that the passing art of geniality among strangers appeared to be alive and well reminding me of another passage in Theroux's *Deep South:*

> "That seemed to be the theme in the Deep South: kindness, generosity, a welcome. I had found it often in my traveling life in the wider world, but I found so much more of it here that I kept going, because the good will was like an embrace. This was utterly unlike the North, or anywhere in the world I'd traveled. 'Raging politeness,' this extreme friendliness is sometimes termed, but even if that is true,

it is better than the cold stare or the averted eyes or the calculated snub I was used to in New England."

Disappointed about news of the closure (and noting the irony of a road called Scenic Drive as being impassable), for a moment I considered disregarding it to see for myself. But as my plan was to avoid backtracking as much as possible, I quickly reconsidered and cashed out at the pump. Picking up the Redwood Highway at an entrance adjacent to Scenic Drive (where a number of cars were indeed exiting – though I had no way of knowing whether they were redirected or simply locals), I followed a forested run so straight and flat that it posted a sixty-five mile-per-hour speed limit – the highest I had seen so far. Although I'm agreeable to any type of woodland drive, this was a far cry from what I was anticipating only moments earlier. However, the scenery changed quickly enough when, after crossing Little River, the walls of fir and spruce opened up to a panoramic view of the Pacific for several, near-sea-level miles along Clam Beach – another posted "Tsunami Hazard Zone."

Upon seeing this most recent sign, I became curious about the history of these seismic events – whether they had actually occurred in this area – and made a note to look into it. By definition a hazard is a danger or risk; a *chance* of something occurring. And in validation of the posted signs, it turns out many of these actually *have* hit the Pacific Northwest in the past 200 years. Further, tsunamis along the west coast of the United States consist primarily of *tele*tsunamis, which are generated by large, very distant earthquakes (more than several hundred miles offshore) as opposed to those closer to land. Two of the most notable teletsunamis occurred in 1946 and 1964 with Crescent City sustaining the most significant damage and having been nearly completely destroyed both times. After learning of this I understood more clearly what Harbor Master Helms meant when he said it's what "Crescent City is known for."

Heading gradually inland through the communities of McKinleyville and Arcata ("big flat place"), the Redwood Highway soon hugged the eastern rim of Arcata Bay and took me west into the port city and county seat of Eureka. Although some travelers may be unimpressed by flat country, there is a certain peacefulness along those open roads; a feeling of space where your mind can relax a bit. Sitting on the shores of Humboldt Bay, the entire city has the unusual distinction of being a state historical landmark for its hundreds of noteworthy Victorian homes including the Carson Mansion (circa 1884); long considered by many architects to be "the most grand Victorian home in America."

Exiting the highway along its merger with the Eel River, I crossed its namesake bridge into a wide expanse of farmlands that soon became very suggestive of the lyrics in Arlo Guthrie's 1972 version of "City of New Orleans." And as I rolled *"along this southbound odyssey... past houses farms and fields,"* I soaked up the miles of open country with the lyrics and chorus running through my mind all the way into Ferndale – a little, old-world, rustic town with its own Victorian homes, community church and western-style, false-fronted businesses... *"Good morning America, how are you? Say, don't you know me? I'm your native son..."*

There's an immediate sense of wonder whenever the landscape changes suddenly and dramatically and the transformation at the edge of Ferndale was no exception. The deep green wall of fir, spruce and tanoak trees rising up at the south end of town is an impressive welcome to the King Range Mountains in the North Coast Ranges – an area characterized to the west by a sharply-rising, wave-cut coastline running almost parallel to the San Andreas Fault all the way down to San Francisco Bay. Veering onto the narrow, two-lane Mattole Road toward Capetown and Petrolia (so named as the site of California's first oil wells), my frame of mind shifted from that relaxed state along the easy and open sea-level drive to a far more focused bearing. And as I became immersed in the alpine landscape, the road ruggedly snaked its way up to nearly 3000 feet. Known locally as "the Wildcat" for the bobcat population living in the area, this wasn't another classic mountain run *between* forested peaks but rather *along* one. A twisting, turning and precarious mountaintop passage with the sort of name that beckons to a traveler… the Lost Coast Highway.

A journal note written during a vista-point stop on my descent into a pocket of mist describes this drive with what I later discovered was near-pinpoint accuracy (albeit before some later Pacific Coast Highway and Topanga Canyon driving succeeded at raising the intensity bar):

> "I feel like I'm in the most remote part of the West Coast right now… driving along the coast with a very rocky shoreline through an extremely thick fog (and feels very chilly outside)… very cool feeling of solitude… just came down the most intense roads there can possibly be."

This steep and challenging stretch of coastline is indeed in the most undeveloped and remote part of California and named the Lost Coast for its relative inaccessibility to the rest of the state. The only coastal wilderness where no major roads come near the ocean, direct access is granted only by way of Mattole Road in Ferndale and its end at Highway 101 nearly eighty miles south. Time seemed to slow down here; the day appearing hesitantly in the works as the distinct and inviting intimacy of the road trip – something not readily found in other forms of travel – continued to captivate me and all but demand that everyday concerns be left behind. A vast and rural landscape left completely intact (save the small roads that afford these views) is a thing of pristine beauty. And as I marveled at the play of light through the trees along miles of winding and deeply wooded runs, I once again felt the serenity of being entirely alone with no immediate end point or timetable other than to finish my drive before sundown. In his book, *Roadshow: Landscape with Drums - A Concert Tour by Motorcycle,* Peart described one of his experiences with this type of unrestricted travel:

"I followed… along the country lanes, through a green world of farms and fields, woods and small settlements. I enjoyed the relaxed pace of having no destination and lots of time to get there."

Equally fascinating were fallen trees that had been cut and removed only where they crossed the road. Driving between the enormous and horizontal sections of trunk that remained on either side like toppled columns offered an entirely new perspective on their age and size; often upwards of 1800 years old and more than twenty feet in diameter. When these woodlands sporadically opened up to less-dense ranges and old cutover land, distant views of the glimmering blue Pacific were just as impressive. Odd to think that so much natural beauty is aligned with the inherent peril of sitting atop some of the most seismically active land in the state. But at that moment, thankfully, all of it remained a calm and isolated magnificence.

Past a few more natural clearings and some obvious manmade ones (evident by dirt tracks and occasional logging trucks) the landscape finally opened up to a sweeping view of the horizon. Miles of twisting, turning thoroughfare looped its way down the foothills ahead of me as the breakers crashed and receded below. This ridgeline run continued south past Capetown, across Bear River and out to Cape Mendocino, both the westernmost point of California and the northernmost end of the nearly 800-mile-long San Andreas Fault. Called the Mendocino Triple Junction, this is where three tectonic plates – the Gorda, North American and Pacific – meet and continually crash into one another. It was here where a downhill switchback brought me to a shoreline straightaway with a farm just to the south where cattle grazed or rested along the roadside fence. It was the first sign of civilization since Ferndale – somewhat unexpected as the entire area seemed otherwise unpeopled. A coastal fog lay low over the mountains just beyond the farm providing a natural cooling and moistening system valuable to the health of the redwoods. And when the steep landscape began to impinge on the coast several miles later, the road climbed inland where another roadside sign attempted to relieve any lingering concerns: "Leaving Tsunami Hazard Zone."

The wonderfully remote and foggy Lost Coast

As I made my way through all these forests, farms and fields, the Lost Coast continued to deliver all manner of delights. And the roads I hoped to discover and travel – those typically driven on only by locals – continued to offer the most in terms of scenery and "inspection of a countryside." To that end, this twisting track through Petrolia and along the Mattole River brought me to the beautiful, rustic, one-lane Honeydew Bridge in the tiny hamlet of Honeydew. Complete with two camelback trusses, spaced timber decking and wooden rails, this weathered 1920 span over the Mattole would be the only such bridge I would cross on this outing. At this realization soon after my trip ended, I looked into it and discovered that it's considered an outstanding example of a "rare and significant bridge type from the early 20th century." Also deemed "functionally obsolete due to geometric constraints, age and seismic susceptibility," at 386 feet it's actually the longest of only three of its kind in existence and, as such, will soon be reconditioned and added to the National Register of Historic Places.

The wonderfully bumpy ride across its wooden tracks was an ideal way to continue my journey – and bring perspective to exactly how agreeably "lost" I was along the secluded and forested back roads of this so-named coast. Although some occasions only seem meaningful or attractive in retrospect, I was very clearly recognizing and fully appreciating the beauty of these moments as they happened. Theroux wrote similarly about the reward of spending time in the far reaches of the Hawaiian island of Molokai in *Fresh Air Fiend:*

> "This forbidden place… had become, because of its very isolation, a place of magic. That is probably the way of the world: a place is preserved as wilderness because it is too inaccessible – too far, too hidden, too maddening to visit, with a rocky coast buffeted by wild weather… beautiful and impossible."

On the threshold of a bridge less traveled

With no further coastal roads for more than eighty miles, I headed northeast on a mostly winding mountainous trek toward Humboldt Redwoods State Park. This severely elevated section of the Lost Coast Highway was as isolated as its earlier run along the water's edge, but with a different reward – distant and widespread views of open valleys and adjacent peaks. Rounding inner mountainside tracks and open outlooks – often without guardrails – offered views both exhilarating and intimidating. Seeing an upcoming stretch of bending road across the valley or a series of switchbacks leading all the way down to the Redwood Highway were matchless in their grandeur and the idea of eventually visiting my view was always intriguing. Although concerns about blind curves to my left were eased slightly by the advantage of that same distant view, the tree line on my right was surprisingly deceptive; rooted one-hundred feet or more below the embankment just outside my passenger door. All striking reminders of the precariousness of these roads… another reason I chose to drive them. After conquering the downhill switchbacks, I welcomed the change of pace offered by the valley floor's far more conservative route – an ideal prelude to one of only a handful of roads I made a specific point of including on this journey.

Passing under the highway at Weott, I picked up an anticipated run along the Avenue of the Giants; a thirty-two-mile, scenic two-lane with the dual distinction of passing through the largest remaining stand of virgin redwoods in the world and of being home to the tallest living tree on the planet. Named after the Greek titan Hyperion ("the high one"), at nearly 380 feet it stands seventy-five feet taller than the Statue of Liberty. It's no wonder American author and poet Mary Hunter Austin wrote that these giants "speak, no doubt, only to the austere mountain heads, to the mindful wind and the watching stars."

Originally built for stagecoaches in the 1880s, this winding path beneath centuries-old canopies was a shaded and tranquil respite from that earlier, more adventuresome trek. There is not much sunlight at the bottom of the redwood forest and this only added to its primeval mystique. Stopping a few miles in simply to stand among these giants (and perhaps to subconsciously test Bryson's assessment of the woods' effect), I indeed felt surrounded and small, though neither confused nor vulnerable, as he wrote. Just more at peace in nature's near-perfect version of silence. This perhaps one aspect of the Japanese practice of shinrin-yoku ("forest bathing"); reconnecting with nature by taking in the atmosphere of the forest through our senses.

Looking around through the maze of trees and finally straight up the furrowed and fibrous bark of an enormous trunk; through the crown of branches and leaves up to whatever I could see of its leader – the topmost part of a tree – was equally mesmerizing and intimidating. It was not unlike a similar view from the foot of a city skyscraper, although its antithesis in every other way. In his 1888 book *Picturesque California* Scottish-American environmentalist and writer John Muir wrote of the redwood's size and standing among its woodland peers:

> "There is something wonderfully telling and impressive about sequoia, even when beheld at a distance of several miles. Its dense foliage and smoothly rounded outlines enable us to recognize it in any company, and when one of the oldest patriarchs attains full stature on some commanding ridge it seems the very god of the woods."

Walking the forest floor added some depth to the experience and I understood even more why these redwoods are so celebrated and sought out by travelers – they're endlessly captivating. Former radio journalist Ketzel Levine said of this thin coastal strip of redwoods: "To describe their beauty is to miss their menace; to speak of their size is to miss their grace."

About to practice some shinrin-yoku

After nearly thirty minutes of this silent meditation of sorts, I felt content enough to return to my Jeep where a quiet soundtrack of classic rock aligned with and sustained that peaceful, easy feeling. As I rejoined the Redwood Highway at the Avenue's end (and after some failed attempts to find available rooms along the way), the music helped set the stage for what turned out to be the day's final leg into Garberville – my cautiously optimistic (or idealistic) view being that any place ending in "ville" must be welcoming and sure to have available cabins or rooms. And as I exited the highway and rolled into this little town nestled in a forested pocket along the Eel River, John Mellencamp's 1985 ode to the quaint simplicity of small-town life ("Small Town") seemed almost too well timed. But that didn't stop me from singing along.

My immediate impression of *this* small town, however, was that there appeared to be an unusually large number of people walking the streets, hanging out on corners or sitting on the sidewalks – their backs against the walls of local businesses. A closer inspection revealed a mix of acoustic guitars, small djembe drums and bongos among the many gatherers – with dreadlocks, tie-dyed shirts and flowing skirts a common theme throughout. As a musician, that overall visual and the apparent musical connection certainly intrigued me. But in those initial moments the loitering aspect on such a grand and stagnant scale seemed to conceal whatever charms this little town had to offer and it made me wonder what was going on. In his 2006 book *Landscape and Race in the United States* American professor and writer Richard Schein noted a similar and prevailing opinion. Expressed in a very straightforward and concise manner by residents of a small town in Westchester County, New York, it was their assertion that "loitering takes away from the village." Be that as it may, I would soon learn that there was both a reason and a silver lining to its occurrence in Garberville.

Finding the small and rustic Humboldt Redwoods Inn at the very south end of town, I managed to book the last available room – both by the manager's say and as evident by his turning away of an older couple who walked in behind me. This, of course, contrary to the reverse timing back at the Oregon border where my first experience with this carefree approach of "no plan, no prospects, no problem" was, well… a problem. Further, it seemed my assessment of the streets was accurate as the manager informed me that the 33rd yearly "Reggae on the River Festival" benefitting a local non-profit community center was in town beginning the following day. So it seemed the loitering would be short lived but the benefits would last; those charms at least somewhat revealed.

Although room availability (and rates) reflected the crowded conditions in Garberville, my plan to wing it worked out well this time as I was able to end my day without having to look for a bed in the next town. As I quietly reassured myself prior to setting out on this excursion (and as I reminded myself each day), *"Don't be surprised if things go wrong, but be grateful when they turn out well."* Perhaps a suitable approach to life as well.

Pleased to be off the road with enough time to settle in before nightfall,

43

I grabbed a bite to eat only a short walk from the hotel, called Kell to catch up on her day and then opened my journal to reflect on my own. There is a lot to observe along the miles – especially when the plan is to put pen to paper later. It's a subtle balance between merely enjoying the scenery as it passes and truly taking it all in (enjoyable but *draining*). Indeed Theroux believed that "the job of the travel writer is to go far and wide, make voluminous notes and to tell the truth… there is immense drudgery in the job."

Even though brief keyword notes taken throughout the day are certainly helpful, my in-motion handwriting leaves a lot to be desired. As such, some of these scribblings take a few minutes or more to decipher. So it's this "time of recount" that is most important. Well… that and sleep. As long as there's enough time and energy for homework when the driving is done and a place to rest my head at the end of each day, I'm fairly well and content.

As Mellencamp sings… *"My bed is in a small town, oh and that's good enough for me…"*

FOUR
Highway 1 Revisited

Let us search the old highways

~ Hilda Doolittle

As morning unfolded, would-be concert goers began to mill about the streets and sidewalks of Garberville (many likely still out from the night before) as I headed toward the overpass near the center of town. And after gassing up the Jeep – something done at nearly every opportunity given my mostly off-the-beaten-path travels – I merged onto the Redwood Highway one last time. Winding my way through that sleepy valley and out of town, I avoided the roadside attractions Confusion Hill and The Legend of Bigfoot and welcomed what appeared to be the start of another beautiful driving day. After a few miles under clear blue skies (and despite record rainfall and mudslides along this part of the coast only six months earlier), I realized that I'd given no consideration to the potential for bad weather – an absence of thought with no consequence as Mother Nature seemed to be cooperating quite nicely.

As the redwoods became denser and the road more tortuous, the speed limit slowed to forty miles per hour and the signs once again announced their warnings: "Rough Road Ahead" and "Tight Curves Next Several Miles." Continuing along these cautioned bends as they followed the South Fork Eel River into Mendocino County, I reveled in the rise and fall of the road as its "tight curves" rounded mountains and crossed bridges wherever the river snaked back and forth beneath the highway. Occasional vista points offered long-range views all the way down into the small community of Leggett where I would finally close out my time on the Redwood Highway and pick up a long-awaited reunion with another storied two-lane course.

My maiden voyage on California State Route 1 – the Pacific Coast Highway (PCH) – some thirty-four years prior was by all accounts as memorable as it should have been. With new challenges, vulnerabilities and views it raised the bar from that earlier Highway 17 experience and quickly reinforced an emerging attraction to scenic driving. That it was also at the other end of my first and equally memorable trip by airplane – the intensity of an unfamiliar ground speed, the smoothness of that "wheels up" moment and a banking-turn, skewed-view of the landscape – simply added to the appeal. Although I've revisited other sections of the PCH in subsequent years (once with my friend, Kevin, which resulted in a long-running joke about speeding along perilous curves and wheels coming off their rims), there would be a nearly twenty-five-year gap between visits.

Leggett may well be considered the epitome of a one-horse town. With its single gas station, school, grocery store and restaurant (and not a stop light to be found), this former logging community likely offers little to the casual traveler aside from Chandelier Tree – the southernmost of

46

three drive-through coastal redwoods in California. Even though I'm usually inclined to avoid this type of roadside attraction, proximity and curiosity won me over. Further encouraged to support the local economy, I gassed up in town before making the one-mile trek to pay my fee and pass through the 2000-year-old redwood named for its chandelier-like limbs. But Leggett's true allure for me – certainly the reason I added it to my drive – was its distinction as home to the northern terminus of the PCH. Although plans originally called for the highway to extend much further north, they were abandoned to avoid the costs and difficulties of establishing routes through the steep and unstable highlands of the Lost Coast region. As such, its span of nearly 656 miles runs north from Dana Point in Orange County to Leggett in Mendocino County. And even though the complete run is widely referred to as the PCH, there are actually three official designations applied somewhat loosely by location: the Pacific Coast Highway (south), the Cabrillo Highway (central) and the Shoreline Highway (north).

Sunlight peeks through the limbs of Chandelier Tree

Regardless of the different names, one common thread throughout the course was the familiar green "California 1" highway sign – its unique spade shape a nod to the miners who came to the state during the gold rush of 1849. This welcome sight and entrance was to some extent a waypoint for me; a reminder that I had no true destination other than to continually head to another scenic byway. As Emerson said, "… the eye seems to demand a horizon."

Before the first bend in the road another promising sight appeared on the shoulder in bright yellow: "Narrow Winding Road Next 22 Miles." The phrasing alone sounded perfect and conjured up an appealing image of what lay ahead. And while it was clearly intended as a warning, it served as more of a teaser reminding me of something Peart said while mapping out a motorcycle course through the back roads of Idaho during Rush's R40 Tour:

> "When you get on this highway, at the beginning you see: 'Warning - 75 Miles of Winding Road Ahead.' To a motorcyclist this is a *promise*, not a threat."

The promise of *my* sign was soon realized after crossing the South Fork Eel River one last time to vanish among the redwoods. Truly feeling immersed in and part of the scenery (as Peter Gabriel sang in "Solsbury Hill" some miles later), I merged onto a series of hairpin turns and blind curves that made up a large part of this mountain pass. Although somewhat challenging by definition, they were more easily negotiated having the luxury of the road to myself. But as this is not always the case, various signs advised that "Slower Traffic Use Turnouts" and "Delay of Vehicles Illegal - Use Turnouts." It seems the powers that be wisely allowed for the "inconvenience" of timid drivers (and distressed vehicles) on these high and narrow roads by adding open clearings – turnouts – every few miles as the landscape allowed.

Descending from this pass onto a leisurely stretch of the PCH buffered by an oceanfront crest, I continued on through a series of meandering and forested switchbacks before arriving hard against the coast. Stopping along a rocky overlook, I walked to the edge and took in a panoramic view that extended several miles south where the shoreline jutted out into the sea at Ten Mile Dunes and Fort Bragg. A thin layer of cirrus clouds high overhead cut across the pale blue sky blanketing the horizon in a wispy white veil and bringing with it a cool ocean breeze that tempered the heat of the midday sun. Returning to the Jeep I harmonized with Warren Zevon, Todd Rundgren and Bob Seger for several enjoyable miles along the water's edge before more warning signs appeared ("Rough Road"… "Proceed with Caution") and the posted speed limit diminished considerably. After the warned-about twists and turns through steep terrain that encroached from the left and dropped off to the right, the road finally straightened out and leveled off taking me past several large rocks off the coast (all named, I'd later discover) and all the way into the historical and picturesque town of Fort Bragg.

The iconic Pacific Coast Highway

Situated along the Mendocino Coast just beyond the wind-raked ocean bluffs, this rustic, pre-Civil War former garrison town (named for Confederate States Army General Braxton Bragg) is the largest of the small communities that populate the area. A state historical landmark, it has a long and varied history as an Indian reservation (the Pomo tribe), established military post, lumber-and-mill town and commercial fishing port. Its eventual status as a burgeoning residential, commercial and tourist destination began around 1973 when the Union Lumber Company, after purchase by Boise Cascade, ultimately became Georgia Pacific – an organization which donated $6,000,000 worth of California redwood groves to the public in 1969.

The actively working fishing harbor on the Noyo River to the south and the steady stream of people walking along the sidewalks in the center of town seemed to add to Fort Bragg's allure and I decided to stop for lunch. Making my way down Main Street past the Guest House Museum (built from coast redwood as a private residence in 1892) to a building called the Union Lumber Company Store (1912), now a consortium of restaurants, shops and boutiques, I encountered a group of resting bicyclists and overheard one of the older riders comment to a presumably newer member, "We always ride through 'Bragg – it's too nice not to."

Hearing that compelled me to casually insert myself into their moment, without introduction, and ask this apparently frequent visitor if he had any recommendations about good places to eat either in town or nearby. Removing his helmet as he stood alongside his bike, he seemed more than willing to assist sharing that there were "a few good places here... it all depends on what you like."

After his brief overview of local eateries ("... some burger places, seafood spots and a pizza shop around the corner – small place, but great pizza..."), I asked about any sites or places to visit along my run down the coast.

"You shouldn't miss the nice, quiet beach in Little River," he said. Then, looking down coast as if it were within view, he pointed and added, "Just stay on the PCH – a nice easy drive – and you'll come right to it."

More welcome solitude along the open road

My estimation of the town and decision to stop was quickly validated by more of that still-thriving geniality among strangers. After thanking him I walked to the Sea Valley Café where I settled in at a corner table flanked by several framed pictures of local fisherman and their boats as the seemingly shy Ashley took my order. Ignoring the television over the bar, I once again escaped into my Kindle where Muir detailed rather favorably his 1894 experiences with the many and varied highlands in this part of the state in *The Mountains of California*:

> "With rough passages here and there they still make delightful pathways for the mountaineer, conducting from the fertile lowlands to the highest icy fountains, as a kind of mountain streets full of charming life and light, graded and sculptured by the ancient glaciers, and presenting, throughout all their courses, a rich variety of novel and attractive scenery, the most attractive that has yet been discovered in the mountain-ranges of the world."

Several tranquil and "easy" miles later, south of Mendocino, I made sure to take the cyclist's sage advice and stopped in Little River to soak up some sun on the unexpectedly dark gray and fairly coarse sand of Van Damme State Park Beach. A small inlet just off the PCH, it's adjacent to a second-growth redwood forest blanketed by tall, stiff sword ferns and home to the Pygmy Forest Discovery Trail – an expanse of low, stunted trees and shrubs. Quiet and peaceful – as described – this obviously dog-friendly alcove was similar to many others tucked away on this ragged and rocky coastline and the sounds of shallow waters lapping at the sand tested my resolve not to drift off. Some time later, having passed that test, I rather reluctantly left the beach to get back behind the wheel and continue on. Heading south through an alternating mix of deeply forested and open landscape I approached Albion Cove where a sign stated simply: "Narrow Bridge." Thankfully an open bend in the road allowed for a clear view of what was actually an enormous, impressive and impending wooden framework that spanned the river between steep bluffs on either side. Carrying the highway across, it was both an unexpected and welcome sight – another unique, two-lane bridge to cross – and I was quick to make a journal note for follow up later.

Built in 1944 toward the end of World War II, the Albion River

Bridge was constructed primarily of salvaged wood due to the shortage of concrete and steel at the time. Even though it was more recently considered functionally obsolete for its restricted width and rail design, plans to replace it were put on an indefinite hold when residents opposing the replacement were successful in their bid to have it listed on the National Register of Historic Places (a designation which became official only days before my crossing). Safe from demolition as of this writing, the 970-foot-long span is the only remaining wooden bridge along the PCH.

Heading inland at the mouth of the Navarro River (blocked by a sandbar on this day), the PCH intersects with Highway 128 before crossing the river and continuing south along the coast. Opting to take in some of the North Coast wine country on my way to connect with an old friend northeast of Sacramento, I followed this former Navarro Highway upriver into Navarro River Redwood State Park and eventually through the remote and sprawling patchwork of the Anderson Valley vineyards. Often referred to as the "redwood tunnel to the sea" for its lengthy canopy of leaves, this meandering, two-lane run through second-growth redwoods also revealed the occasional clearing where imposing shale outcroppings loomed high and the contrasting river flowed peacefully along the southbound side. Occasional swing gates flanking the road with attached "Stop," "Road Closed" and "Flooded" signs were evidence of the river's capacity to rise in rainy weather – typically when the sandbar isn't breached. The sight of these gates returned my thoughts to images of those February downpours which made so many California roads impassable – any "dramatic" appeal of that weather certainly lost at that point. As one of my previously noted objectives was to avoid any backtracking or repetition, the thought of having to unexpectedly retreat after coming this far renewed my appreciation for the picture-perfect weather I was experiencing.

When Highway 128 wandered from the river several miles east, the woods seemed to simultaneously close in even tighter allowing only dappled sunlight to reach the road (the Japanese, whose deep appreciation of nature is reflected in the many words they have for it, refer to this type of scattered light as *komorebi*). Fallen trees dotted the forest floor (I wondered if they made a sound); their remaining trunks either cut level or left jagged. Nearing Navarro, post-and-wire fences ran sporadically along stretches of open landscape where old rustic sheds stood roadside every few miles; each abandoned, some moss covered and one caving in on itself. Each its own little story, I thought. As the towering redwood, fir and oak trees began to thin and give way to a pastoral view of gently sloping hills, the light fell more freely and I was greeted warmly and fittingly by an engraved wooden sign: "Anderson Valley Welcomes You."

Komorebi through the redwoods

Once little more than a series of stagecoach stops en route to the coast, this section of the nearly 140-mile highway would make Dionysus proud. Known as Wine Road – and for good reason – it rolls straight through the heart of the Napa, Sonoma and Mendocino wine regions (or more formally AVAs – American Viticultural Areas) passing dozens of wineries, vineyards and cellars along the way. Unfamiliar with the differences among those designations at the time of my visit (figuring they were all somewhat interchangeable), I noted it as a homework assignment for later (Winery: a property that produces wine... Vineyard: a plantation where grapes are grown for wine... Cellar: a place for storing and aging wine).

Far-reaching views of evenly spaced trellises topped with deep-green and dark-blue canopies of grapes in veraison all set against a backdrop of golden hills and Coast Ranges pointed to the valley's allure. Further characterized by its remoteness and its proximity to the Pacific's marine influence on its climate, this waypoint stop for me seemed an equally likely and ideal weekend destination. Calling the road my own for several miles, I was able to casually observe a handful of wineries before the beautifully landscaped Navarro Vineyards & Winery caught my eye. A large and colorful bed of dahlias, peonies and snapdragons on the near side of the entrance balanced by a run of red roses bordering a zig-zag, split-rail fence on the far side lured me in for a closer look. The striking, dark redwood exterior of the barnlike tasting room stood out among all others I passed that day and I decided to make this my Anderson Valley wine stop.

After a brief discussion with a wine server about the valley's history (grapes were first grown here in the mid-1800s), its landscape (comprised of more than 15,000 acres) and even Navarro's tasting room (built from fallen redwoods on the property), I ordered a few bottles of Pinot Grigio and Pinot Gris to be shipped home to Kell before stepping outside to relax for a while on the wraparound deck. This quiet and picturesque view of the rolling hills and manicured grapevines seemed almost as essential to the vineyard as the wine itself and was a welcome respite from the road. And even though that road had shown many rewards so far, it was always good to stop and smell the roses, redwoods and even the grapes as these and other settings seemed as therapeutic for the mind as for the eye. But once again, well rested and visually content, the occasional and enthusiastic approach of *"What next?"* resurfaced and I was soon on my way.

The view for miles along Wine Road

As I continued past the fruit stands and apple orchards that dotted the southbound side of Wine Road (apples, peaches and pears were some of the original crops of the valley), the distinctive voice of the Doobie Brothers' Michael McDonald contributed to the soundtrack of my journey. Although a song about unrequited love, the chorus to "What a Fool Believes" seems to serve equally well as commentary on the unquestionable wonder that embodies all these back roads and coastal drives... *"What a fool believes he sees, no wise man has the power to reason away."* Further, just as another's account of the same outing would be entirely his or her own, all that this (reluctant) "fool" has described on these pages has been – and could only be – exclusively my perspective; my understanding. Once again in *Travels with Charley,* Steinbeck explains this singular perception and ownership of our experiences:

> "I feel that there are too many realities. What I set down here is true until someone else passes that way and rearranges the world in his own style. In literary criticism, the critic has no choice but to make over the victim of his attention into something the size and shape of himself. And in this report I do not fool myself into thinking I am dealing with constants. For this reason I cannot commend this account as an America you will find. So much there

is to see, but our morning eyes describe a different world than do our afternoon eyes, and surely our wearied evening eyes can report only a weary evening world."

Just south of Boonville where the sparsely populated Anderson Valley ends and its floor opens up to an even less inhabited expanse of yellow grasses and farmlands, a sign cautioned: "Speed Enforced by Radar." While the open-road view was far and wide with no other cars in sight (law enforcement or otherwise), there was no persuasive desire on my part to disregard the posted fifty-five-mile-per-hour speed limit any more than I already had been. This was just as well as beyond a few remaining hillside vineyards the open flatlands transitioned to beautifully mountainous terrain. This stretch of Highway 128 slowly wound its way up to more than 1000 feet before descending into the Bay Area by way of Sonoma County along a shaded bend in the road. Labeled a "Safety Corridor" by a roadside sign that further advised to "Drive Safely," I became curious about this designation and another journal note was made.

It seems that "safety" was an optimistic term – perhaps a Department of Transportation version of a hopeful self-fulfilling prophecy. According to the Transportation Safety Resource Center, this label is assigned to an area or a segment of highway based on its "increased accident rates, fatalities and traffic volume," among other criteria (probably best I didn't know this earlier). Further, it was noted that these roads "experienced a crash rate of fifty percent over the state average and have sustained 1000 or more crashes over a three-year period." Based on all that unsettling information, I was surprised not to have seen more of these signs peppered throughout the coast.

I deliberately avoided researching any statistics like that before beginning this trip (though I did quite a bit afterwards) because the plan was to stay off the beaten path. And inherent in that is an expectation of occasionally driving on roads which would likely not be very hospitable or effortlessly navigable. As a travel-genre enthusiast I was well aware that I wasn't negotiating anything like Bolivia's single-lane North Yungas Highway ("Death Road") or even the no-guardrail, hairpin curves of the Million Dollar Highway in Colorado – both above the 11,000-foot mark. But there were plenty of back roads on my journey offering both elevation and adventure in good measure – some written about on previous pages and others coming up. As such, there was no need to unnecessarily alarm myself with unnerving information. Because (and at the risk of imbuing the vague and pithy "it is what it is") the trip was being taken regardless.

The warning to drive safely resonated immediately, however, as a series of twists, turns and switchbacks wound me even further down into Cloverdale ("Where the Vineyards Meet the Redwoods," according to a sign at the town's entrance). And although still trying to avoid the "high-speed slashes of concrete and tar," I reluctantly merged onto The 101 south toward San Francisco with an eventual destination that would focus on a different type of landscape.

The small towns of Asti, Geyserville and Healdsburg were essentially a collage of patchwork fields. Neatly lined rows of grapevines like viticultural soldiers standing at attention ran both parallel and perpendicular to the highway and led me directly to the county seat of Santa Rosa ("Saint Rose" of Lima – the patroness saint of gardeners and florists) where I decided to call it a day. The somewhat extensively named but pleasant-sounding Best Western Plus Wine Country Inn & Suites would prove a very comfortable home for the night. And after walking to a nearby restaurant for a simple dinner, I returned to my room to write, read and relax. Little did I know that fewer than two months later much of the area I was in would be ravaged by one of the most destructive wildfires in California's history (tragically to be outdone by several other massive and deadly fires over the course of the next few years).

Dubbed the Northern California Firestorm, it was a series of fires which devastated 245,000 acres and nearly 9000 structures in parts of Napa, Lake, Sonoma, Mendocino, Butte and Solano Counties. Destroying more than 1000 homes and businesses only two blocks west of my hotel (to include the restaurant where I ate) and nearly 5700 structures across 37,000 acres, the Tubbs Fire – named for its origin near Tubbs Lane in neighboring Calistoga – was the single most destructive fire ever in the state to date. Beyond the heart-wrenching and irreparable human toll, these events have wide-ranging effects on both wildlife and landscape; repercussions of which take several years to reverse.

Most of us don't give much thought to the roads we drive on every day unless they're closed for repairs or otherwise rendered impassable. That my trip through this landscape followed flooding rains and road-closing mudslides and preceded the conflicting tragedy of devastating wildfires that caused mass evacuations was, at the very least, a sobering thought. As such, I feel very fortunate to have been able to drive the many back roads and take in all the pristine scenery of those mostly coastal state parks and small towns at a time when Mother Nature wasn't so intent on evening the odds.

FIVE

Musical Landscapes

Music is the language of the spirit

~ Kahlil Gibran

As opposed to the reasons for all my previous planned trips to California – to carouse with friends, reside for a brief period of time or even celebrate my first wedding anniversary – it was a leisurely, meandering and intimate solo drive down the coast that brought me here this time. A desire to "contemplate wood and water and the quick-rising mountains with crowns of conifers and the fir trees high up," as Steinbeck wrote. To temporarily break from my east-coast routine and more closely examine the landscape of this west-coast state of which I became so enamored nearly thirty-five years ago.

Perhaps this was just one of the whispers of approaching age. The need to check off a box on a bucket list that never existed. To once more "go west, young man" – however brief or mellow that visit may be – in an effort to prevent any delay from becoming a missed opportunity. Whatever the deep-seated reason, as with many other personal interests I knew for certain that it was very closely tied to and even partially inspired by an equally rooted and lifelong passion for music.

With the temperature hovering around seventy degrees when I stepped out onto my terrace, my immediate thought was *"Summertime in Santa Rosa."* The words had a lyrical ring so I jotted them down with thoughts of adding them to all the other titles and verses of songs I no longer seem to complete. As the sun seemingly kept the clouds at bay, the blue sky, warm air and distinct quiet of daybreak settled over me and I sat at the table for some early morning journaling. Although typically happy to complete this task and turn the page at the end of each day – fairly optimistic that memory and notes have served me well – "unconscious processing" (or so I've read) occasionally finds me with at least a few more details to capture on paper by morning. In this telling, I'm reminded of a simple but vivid passage by American writer Ernest Hemingway about a similarly promising start to a day in Paris in his 1926 novel *The Sun Also Rises*:

> "In the morning I walked down the Boulevard to the rue Soufflot for coffee and brioche. It was a fine morning. The horse-chestnut trees in the Luxembourg gardens were in bloom. There was the pleasant early-morning feeling of a hot day. I read the papers with the coffee and then smoked a cigarette."

What seemed to be a typical day weather-wise was actually a bit of an anomaly as most of California was in the middle of what turned out to be a five-month, record-breaking heatwave. Contributing immeasurably to the recent Northern California Firestorm, this increasingly common "feeling of a hot day" and overall rise in temperatures has long been cause for concern among climate-control scientists who speculate it may soon become the state's new norm – likely to the frustration of many residents. As for this visitor and backroad traveler, however (and perhaps a bit selfishly), it was hard not to consider these conditions ideal.

My morning routine complete, I closed the door on Santa Rosa, fueled up the Jeep and disposed of several unappealing miles along The 101 before an off-ramp led me to a far more scenic route to the coast. By design and preference, it was the long way around to my next stop and did not disappoint. The open flatlands, old weathered barns and failing split-rail fences heading west were like a Norman Rockwell painting come to life. The cadence of Led Zeppelin's version of "When the Levee Breaks" helped set the mood of the road and my driving and thoughts relaxed in equal measure as I sang along... *"If it keeps on rainin', the levee's going to break..."*

When a sign advised of a "Congested Area" ahead, I became curious about what that could possibly mean in the middle of all this "nowhere" in Petaluma – originally the village of Péta Lúuma when home to some tribes of the indigenous Coast Miwok people who, I would soon discover, inhabited many areas along the northern California coast. With the exception of a beautiful, old and somewhat historic roadhouse-turned-restaurant (Washoe House - 1859), it was a curiosity that essentially went unanswered as there was little more up the road than my next turn toward the coast. Bordered by native grasses later identified as blue wildrye and purple needlegrass (the official state grass of California – naturally able to withstand drought and summer heat), this westerly run was blissfully all mine on this day. And as I rolled quietly along past sprawling farms with working ranches and outbuildings all set back from the road, farmhands worked the fields, the sun continued its assault undiffused and my relaxed frame of mind remained the same... *"Cryin' won't help ya, prayin' won't do you no good..."*

63

Miles of open pastures and skies eventually returned me to an inland stretch of the PCH just west of Bloomfield where it crossed into the affluent and storied Marin County (named for Chief Marin of the Licatiut tribe of the Coast Miwok). Established in 1850 just months before the state was admitted to the Union, this southerly peninsula ultimately connected with San Francisco by way of the Golden Gate Bridge and proved as visually appealing as would be expected; the Pacific Ocean to the west and both the San Francisco and San Pablo Bays to the east. Winding southwest through rolling hills and coastal mountains, the road quickly settled along the eastern bank of a tranquil-looking Tomales Bay – a description which belies any evidence of the San Andreas Fault's submerged and potentially perilous run down its center (only one of countless faults throughout the state to include the San Jacinto fault at its southern end). The sight of several birds of varying size and color was itself a thing of beauty. Whether flocking in symmetrical and graceful flight against the bright blue sky or floating effortlessly on the dark still waters, they added to the scene's allure and piqued my curiosity enough to make a few notes.

As it turns out, this fifteen-mile-long tidal estuary supports more than fifty species of water fowl – thirteen of which are threatened or endangered. Among the many types said to nest or winter in this extensively studied and well-protected area are Black Brant Geese, Savannah Sparrows and the rarely seen Yellow Rail – its feathers boasting a stunning tiger-striped look. One of the most secretive birds in North America, its call is heard almost exclusively at night.

At the southernmost end of the bay sits Point Reyes Station, a former port and railway terminus east of the windswept bluffs of the Point Reyes National Seashore. It was here where I once again opted off the PCH and headed inland to a planned destination in the county seat of San Rafael. A winding and forested ridgeline route over the placid waters of the Nicasio Reservoir brought me to the gently sloping valley of its namesake town where I was immediately taken in by more Rockwell-esque scenery. A one-room schoolhouse (Nicasio School - 1871) and an old country church complete with steeple and built from local redwoods (Old St. Mary's of Nicasio Valley - 1867) were nestled among the wide-open backdrop of rolling horse farms and stables. Some homes sat hard against the shoulder of the road behind wooden fences with swing gates as various flags hung motionless from their poles. Stopping briefly to decide on a path forward, I pulled into the dirt parking lot of a modest but well-maintained Little League field. Its wooden bleachers and dugouts – all empty on this day – spoke well to Nicasio's old-world charm. I imagined eventful summer weekends; games being played, busy concession stands selling hot dogs and soft drinks and young players all "Choosin' Up" (as in Rockwell's so-named 1951 painting) and awaiting their turn at bat while dreaming of the big leagues. It was precisely that kind of town – a slice of Americana. Small, endearing and well worth the stop.

The meandering two-lane blacktop continued out of town rambling on for several peaceful miles as an ever-changing landscape eventually offered another version of scenic finery. Where a dense timberland of firs, redwoods and oaks sporadically opened up, sweeping easterly views took over and promised what appeared to be a beautiful valley in the distance. As the road began steadily descending into the town of San Rafael, the north shore of the glistening San Francisco Bay came more fully into view and my journey's focus on the natural landscape quickly shifted to one a bit more music related.

Both historically and artistically rich and diverse, Marin County boasts an assortment of music halls, theater companies and art galleries all set against a rural landscape of cattle ranches, houseboat communities and roadhouses. Even San Quentin Prison (1854), one of the oldest and most well-known penitentiaries in the country (as referenced in numerous TV shows, movies, songs and books) resides on the bay just north of San Francisco – somewhat ironically facing the small harbor community of Paradise Cay. And just as with Pelican Bay State Prison back in Crescent

65

City, I'd soon learn that San Quentin sat in stark contrast to its immediate surroundings.

But Marin's most notable structure is very likely the Marin County Civic Center – noted architect Frank Lloyd Wright's last major project and his only realized government entity. Its low-level, open-space design was part of Wright's plan to have it "melt into the sunburnt hills" that surround it earning it both admiration and eventual designation as a National Historic Landmark (1991). With its iconic circular design and blue-domed roof, one of the most identifiable accessory buildings in the Civic Center complex is the nearby and relatively small, 2000-seat Marin Veterans' Memorial Auditorium. And as with the Civic Center's highly regarded status and recognition within architectural circles, only five years after its 1971 opening the Memorial Auditorium played an integral part in the history of rock'n'roll.

Marin Veterans' Memorial Auditorium *Comes Alive!*

Long before the pervasiveness of YouTube and myriad other Internet downloading and streaming services placed live music and video footage so readily at our fingertips, bands would release live albums to showcase their concert performances – particularly in the 1970s and '80s. On occasion when these albums would strike just the right chord with fans, sales would equal or surpass those of many studio releases – sometimes becoming an artist's best-selling effort. Bob Seger & the Silver Bullet Band shot to new heights with the success of *Live Bullet* in 1976 – an album recorded at Cobo Hall in Seger's hometown of Detroit, Michigan. Venturing a bit further from their Rockford, Illinois home, Cheap Trick broke through in America by way of Tokyo, Japan and their biggest-selling album – 1978's *At Budokan*. And The Rolling Stones (*Get Yer Ya-Ya's Out* - 1970), Jackson Browne (*Running On Empty* - 1977) and U2 (*Under A Blood Red Sky* - 1983) all attained critical acclaim and widely broadened fan bases as a direct result of their early live concert releases. But never has the formula been proven more successfully than when Peter Frampton stepped onto the stage of the Marin Veterans' Memorial Auditorium in June of 1975.

A former member of British bands The Herd and Humble Pie, Frampton was a nine-year veteran of the music business at the time with four solo albums under his belt, only modest success and no hit singles. But by the time his set ended approximately sixty minutes later, he had unwittingly started a series of shows that would eventually jumpstart his solo career and firmly establish him as "the next big thing" in rock'n'roll.

Crossing into San Rafael and approaching the venue, a familiar and anticipatory sense of being in that place where something noteworthy happened began to wash over me and, as always, I was intent on remaining in the moment. Quietly hoping chance would favor me in the form of a Frampton song on the radio (it didn't), I crossed over The 101 and found my way to the entrance at the Avenue of the Flags where a striking war memorial "To All Who Served" was immediately to my left. Out of curiosity and reverence I stopped to read all seven monuments representing Army, Navy, Air Force, Marine, Coast Guard and Merchant Marine personnel who gave their lives in World War II, Korea, Vietnam, Iraq and Afghanistan. I found this reminder of their service and our freedoms to be far more moving – though no less real – than passing by prisons. As such, it was a welcome and worthwhile pause in my day. Eventually parking just outside the venue and taking it all in, I was soon inside – in that place – and doing the same.

67

Within three months of its January 1976 release, the double-live album *Frampton Comes Alive!* was at the top of the Billboard charts along with other notable efforts by some of rock'n'roll's elite. The Eagles (*Greatest Hits*), Led Zeppelin (*Presence*), The Rolling Stones (*Black and Blue*) and Wings (*Wings at the Speed of Sound*) were all taking turns sitting at Number One that spring. And after hitting that top spot early on then quickly dropping back, *'Comes Alive!* landed there much more firmly in July and proceeded to own the rest of the Bicentennial summer and early fall on the heels of "Baby, I Love Your Way," "Do You Feel Like We Do" and "Show Me The Way." To put the success of the album in perspective, it took Stevie Wonder's *Songs in the Key of Life* to end Frampton's reign.

Entering the arena, I reflected on those acclaimed live versions introduced to me by way of my older sister Diane's album and turntable. I thought about how widely known they are around the world and, more specifically, how they originated here... *in this place.* I imagined the audience members from that time – more than forty years ago – passing through those same doors unaware they were about to become a fairly significant part of the biggest-selling live album in history (as were audiences from three subsequent shows at Winterland Ballroom in San Francisco, Long Island Arena in Commack, New York and Memorial Hall in Plattsburgh, New York). During a mixing session at Hollywood's A&M Studios prior to the album's release, Frampton told then-Rolling Stone Contributing Editor Cameron Crowe about the impact those crowds had both on the shows and on the album:

> "We have a good time onstage 'cause we realize it gets through to the audience. Listen to them! They want to be entertained. And when I'm applauded for doing that, all it makes me want to do is entertain more. They are as much a part of this record as anybody."

With only an unanticipated and quick glimpse into the actual auditorium (denied further access by a security guard neither impressed nor swayed by my feeble explanation that I planned to write about it), the stage appeared no bigger than that of my high school and I had to soak up whatever atmosphere I could from the atrium. Having long wondered about that arena (and others from other bands' live albums) and having finally seen it, an element of contentedness settled in and I eventually left the building to stroll around the well-manicured grounds to take it all in from a broader perspective. A short time later I continued my southbound journey in silence, those songs and imagined footage of a time long past still playing loudly and vividly in my head as the arena gradually receded in my rearview mirror... *"Must have been a dream, I don't believe where I've been, come on, let's do it again..."*

Of course, getting to that always-sought-after "somewhere else" continued to be part of the plan. But getting there *quickly* was not. As Steinbeck wrote: "The small wood roads, they are not conducive to speed." As such, they were the obvious draw for me. What they cost in time was more than repaid in enjoyment. So when I discovered my next planned destination was fewer than twenty miles away, a longer and more indirect route was in order. Something more consistent with my preference for the most scenic way around, over or through (coupled with my appreciation for anticipation).

After leaving the grounds of the Memorial Auditorium and almost immediately being faced with the dismal prospect of once again having to take The 101, an impromptu westerly run along surface roads found me happily climbing and twisting my way through some promising narrow and tree-lined streets. Further discovery of a slow and meandering path through Boyd Memorial Park was a bonus, its lush green foliage shading the way and further encouraging me to press on. Learning later that the Boyd family was connected to the original 1874 settlement of the City of

San Rafael only added color to the experience. But a few miles later, as the promise of this alternate route was settling in, it was just as quickly broken in a mazelike series of endless loops and congested residential dead ends – some quite literally – as gates crossed roads in the middle of the day despite signs indicating "Open Space: Closed Sunset to Sunrise."

My efforts at finding a "longcut" (as I refer to my more indirect routes) began to fall away as the hilly terrain just west of nearby San Anselmo and the even more attractive redwoods and oaks of Mount Tamalpais ("Mount Tam" to locals) of the distant North Coast Ranges became seemingly unreachable from any point of origin. Despite all reasonable attempts to once again become pleasantly lost in the landscape, it appeared I was literally at an impasse and caught up in a "can't get there from here" situation. After exhausting all efforts I reluctantly waved the figurative white flag, found an on-ramp to The 101 and set off toward the former World War II shipbuilding town and current artistic residential enclave of Sausalito ("small willow grove").

Compensation for this "concrete and tar" part of my drive came in the form of sporadic views of mountainous greenery to the west near Mill Valley and widespread views of the deep-blue San Rafael and Richardson Bays to the east – both part of San Francisco Bay. More immediately, albeit on a smaller scale, a series of "mission bells" hanging on shepherd's hooks began appearing along the shoulder of the road for the next several miles (and beyond) prompting a journal note and the usual follow-up.

What seemed to be simple and unusual roadside enhancements turned out to be indicators that I was now on the California Mission Trail; a 600-mile stretch of The 101 from Mission Basilica San Diego de Alcalá (1769) to Mission San Francisco Solano (1823). Scholars believe the mission system was an attempt by Spain to convert Native Americans to Catholicism, colonize the region and expand European territory along the Pacific coast. In the decades following the system's end (1833) the missions and their land were in a state of ownership flux before being used briefly as military bases during the Mexican-American war (1846). Today most of these historic structures are tourist attractions with museums. And the trail, known as El Camino Real ("The Royal Road"), is a California Historical Landmark (1959) connecting all twenty-one missions, four presidios and multiple pueblos with mission bells intermittently marking the entire run since 1906.

Once in Sausalito, I was captivated by the harbor view and momentarily went off course to take a brief drive along the water. Far-reaching views of Angel Island, Alcatraz Island ("pelican") and the city of San Francisco brought a new perspective to the vastness and beauty of the Bay Area and, having been away for so long, a renewed appreciation for all of it.

Named by European explorers for the groves of small willow trees that used to populate its banks and creeks, Sausalito has held many identities since its 1838 founding. From a vibrant working-class culture of business owners, railroad workers and ranchers in those early days to a town of fishermen, prohibition-era bootleggers and shipbuilders during World War II, it has seen its cast of characters. But soon after the war effort ended, the ship building stopped and the characters once again changed. The beauty and affordability of this waterfront town attracted a mix of artists, writers, musicians and actors resulting in the emergence of a bohemian counterculture that, despite a long and continued coexistence with more mainstream and affluent professionals, defines Sausalito to this day.

Hidden among a collection of nondescript offices and warehouses along the harbor off Richardson Bay sits a small, low-level building diagonally sided in well-weathered redwood and somewhat camouflaged by the surrounding trees. Distinctive in both current appearance and former purpose, it was the primary reason for my stop in Sausalito. Yet finding it was not without some difficulty and a few wrong turns. But when the large white "2200" over the entrance came into view (familiar from books and videos), I knew my search had ended and I was hopeful that a rendezvous with another piece of California's historical musical landscape was about to begin.

The venerable Record Plant Studio in Sausalito

When The Record Plant opened in Sausalito in October 1972 (John Lennon – with Yoko Ono – among the famous musician attendees at the opening party where the Grateful Dead played), it was the last of three recording studios to bear that name. But it was hardly considered last with regard to producing its share of diverse and noteworthy albums. Although New York's Record Plant (1968) could boast about *Electric Ladyland* (The Jimi Hendrix Experience), *Born to Run* (Bruce Springsteen) and *Toys In the Attic* (Aerosmith) and the Los Angeles studio (1969) counted *Piano Man* (Billy Joel), *Hotel California* (Eagles) and *Out of Order* (Rod Stewart) among its successes, Sausalito represented the name equally well by producing the multi-platinum-selling *Songs in the Key of Life* (Stevie Wonder), *Sports* (Huey Lewis & The News) and *Supernatural* (Santana), among many others. One of those others, with the working title *Yesterday's Gone*, would go on to become one of the best-selling albums of all time under its eventual and more-telling title *Rumours*. It would take British-American rockers Fleetwood Mac to unheralded heights earning them both critical acclaim and a dedicated following that continues to this day.

The limited parking at 2200 Bridgeway (fewer than twenty miles south of where some of *Frampton Comes Alive!* was recorded) belied the studio's prestige. But at the same time it seemed to make perfect sense given its home along this short two-mile haven. Both studio and harbor are relatively small and unassuming in and of themselves, yet both are very integral aspects of their respective landscapes. Approaching the entrance with its famously carved doors (a literal band of animals), I was eager to step inside. But as the studio had been closed since 2008 the doorknob – centered on a tuxedoed fox's bass drum – wouldn't turn. So I found my way to a side door which led to the reception area of Harmonia, a holistic "health and well-being social club" that has occupied one side of the building since 2011. Once inside, an immediate sense of history and solitude was evident in its dim lighting, narrow-wood-lined interior and stone wall accents – most of which appeared beautifully and relatively unchanged since the '70s.

Foxes and owls and bears… *oh my!*

The warm, easy greeting by a woman named Kara (Harmonia's general manager, I would later learn) was both welcome and inspiring. Her overall appearance was strikingly similar to Fleetwood Mac vocalist Stevie Nicks from her younger days in this very place. Tanned and slight, her pretty face casually framed by long, wavy, blonde hair spilling onto her shoulders, she approached as I introduced myself. A relaxed top and long, flowing skirt completed a look that seemed to effortlessly fit the vibe of the room – past and present.

After a bit of small talk, I told Kara of my backroad journey down the coast and my wish to visit the actual studio "where so much great music was written and recorded – to be in that place and to write about it."

"I'm sorry," she said quietly and somewhat regretfully, "but the doors to the rest of the building are locked." Then, as a consolation of sorts, she continued, "But you can look around on this side if you want."

Showing me a few of the unique and narrow halls; one arched along the top, another wavy on both sides, as well as some of the renovated rooms that have been written about – rooms that played their part in the music and stories that were created here – all piqued my interest further. With a sneaking suspicion she may have access to the adjoining rooms, I offered an unassertive plea to be as brief as possible if allowed a further look inside. She looked at me impassively for only a few seconds. But that was enough to immediately remind me how I was "always mindful not to overstay my welcome" whenever backstage at concerts. Those words, which I had written back in 2011 (*From the Inside*), were resonating loudly now. And just as I was about to thank her for her kindness and leave, she broke the silence.

"Five minutes," she quietly said. "I'll give you five minutes to look around and come back out – but you can't turn on the lights and you can't make me come after you."

"I'll be back in five minutes," I assured her without missing a beat.

With that, she grabbed her keys, opened a door to the other side and allowed me a hurried version of a trip back in time. Suddenly all the pictures and footage that I had seen of this place, all the music that so many millions of fans have come to know and appreciate during the past forty-five years (forty of them since *Rumours* was released to the world)… all of that happened here… *in this place.* An oft-used phrase came to mind as I looked around: "If these walls could talk." Only later, when reading those words in my notes, did I realize that nowhere does that phrase ring more truly than in a recording studio where – ostensibly – the walls *do* talk by way of all the music recorded there.

A wavy walk into the depths of the studio

My self-guided tour through some of the windowless studio was not unlike the childhood memory of feeling my way through an amusement park's haunted house; hands on the walls, eyes trying to acclimate to the relative darkness while simultaneously wondering what lay around each corner. Thankfully a small, round "porthole" window in a back door allowed a fair amount of natural light into a central location where doors to some of the main rooms and both studios were situated and where a 1904 Maxfield Parrish print – *Air Castles* – hung alone and somewhat out of place. In his 2012 book *Making Rumours: The Inside Story of the Classic Fleetwood Mac Album,* Grammy Award-winning producer Ken Caillat wrote about that door as well as the studio's unusually sequestered layout and design and the feelings of isolation it created while working on *Rumours*:

> "The connecting hallways were narrow, dark, and uneven, like something out of a Tolkien story. Just outside our studio was a door with a porthole. When we were recording the album, I would often take a break and look through that round window. I wondered what other people were doing, and my sense of separation from the real world would increase. It was like looking out an airplane window while flying over a foreign land."

Although the overall sense was one of abandonment it did not at all seem to be one of neglect. Gold and platinum albums by Heart, Starship and the late Aretha Franklin, among others, on display outside both the studio and control room entrances gave the impression that there was still some life left in these old walls while other indications seemed present in less tangible ways. But Studios A and B with their well-kept parquet floors, high ceilings and wildly painted walls once filled with the sounds of music stood empty, dark and most of all… silent. Foam baffles that caught some of those iconic sounds were either still in place on the walls or neatly stacked against them. And vacant control room windows gazed out at all of this emptiness as silenced playback speakers lingered in place above the long-gone mixing boards (one now owned by Journey keyboardist Jonathan Cain). Given all this scarcity and absence, there was a certain irony to the words of a small blue sign still hanging outside Control Room B: "Record Plant is not responsible for personal property left or stored on our premises."

Where the magic happens and the results are displayed

This is what I had come for and what has always fascinated me to varying degrees… being where the magic had occurred – no matter the focus. As noted on the past several pages, whether in an office building or a home, a concert hall or a parking lot, spending some time where something widely noted or personally significant happened has always added to its appeal by deepening whatever connection may have previously existed. And as all of this is inextricably linked to the nostalgia of looking back – a practice often maligned or misunderstood – it serves well to note that in visiting (or revisiting) these places, memories and moments can be recaptured and restored… or quite simply remembered. In his 2016 autobiography *Born to Run* Bruce Springsteen wrote similarly and fondly about an attempt to reconnect with a "towering" copper beech tree that he would spend hours playing on and around as a boy growing up in Freehold, New Jersey:

> "It was gone but still there. The very air and space above
> it was still filled with the form, soul and lifting presence
> of my old friend, its leaves and branches now outlined and

shot through by evening stars and sky. A square of musty earth, carved into the parking lot blacktop at pavement's edge, was all that remained. It still held small snakes of root slightly submerged by dust and dirt, and there, the arc of my tree, my life, lay plainly visible. My great tree's life by county dictum or blade could not be ended or erased. Its history, its *magic*, was too old and too strong."

Honoring my agreement with Kara, I returned to the reception area within five minutes (give or take). After some final small talk and a handshake, I thanked her for the opportunity as she took a picture of me next to a finely crafted, ten-foot-tall, mock electric guitar leaning against the wall – another remnant from the studio's heyday. Walking out of this dark "secret haven for celebrity musicians," as Caillat referred to it, I had to shade my eyes from the sudden brightness of the early afternoon sun. In doing so, I noticed that a small piece of the angled redwood siding was chipped and slightly sticking out near the bottom of those extraordinary front doors. Bending down, I snapped it off and placed it in my pocket… a small, five-inch piece of musical-landscape history to help inspire a story and to display with other similar memorabilia nearly 3000 miles away in a South Jersey room devoted to all things music.

Once again driving off in silence – *Rumours* on my mental playlist this time – I headed north along the harbor, the picturesque view of boats on the bay serving well as a lasting impression of Sausalito. And as an on-ramp to The 101 led me away my long-term memory subconsciously began working its own type of magic as thoughts of my visit to both town and studio continued to resonate in song… *"Thunder only happens when it's raining, players only love you when they're playing…"*

My next planned stop was a diversion from the mostly backroad southerly route I had kept to so far. But it was more than welcome and willingly taken. Crossing an inlet off Richardson Bay – the San Francisco skyline and the iconic Golden Gate Bridge clearly visible to the south – I continued

79

northeast for several relatively uneventful miles hoping to find another scenic route that would take me at least some of the way there (a hope unrealized). But regardless of direction or distance, when a long-anticipated reunion with an old friend is on the horizon, any road is a good one.

SIX

Familiar Faces

A journey is best measured in friends rather than miles

~ Tim Cahill

As a young drummer moving to northern California in 1984 I was armed with fair and equal amounts of talent, eagerness and ambition… but even more naiveté. And after working with a handful of bands over the course of a year and finding even fewer promising opportunities, that early west-coast version of my musical aspirations proved short lived. On the other hand, my friendship with high school classmate and Sacramento roommate Scot remained stronger than ever. And so it was that on this journey nearly thirty-three years later a deviation from my scenic-only travel plan was not only considered… it was considered essential.

Citrus Heights (its slogan: "Solid Roots - New Growth") was an out-of-the-way break in my run; an inland trek slightly more than 120 miles northeast of the coast. But with the rewarding expectation of some downtime for writing and an overdue reconnection with an old friend, it was eagerly anticipated. Although it would have been easier to have carried on unencumbered by any self-imposed demands on my time; to have allowed the road to continue leading me wherever it may and to let the stories fall more easily onto the page, that was not the case with this diversion. Nor did I want it to be. And even though my search continued for that always-preferable, long and roundabout scenic route, each passing mile diminished any chances of finding one and I ultimately (begrudgingly) surrendered to the shortest distance between two points.

In *Travels with Charley* Steinbeck briefly remarked about a similar detour he had taken during the 1960 journey throughout America which informed his book. He dismissed this planned but outlying stop in Chicago to meet with his wife as having no literary value to his readers. And when it came time for inclusion in the story, he held firm to this opinion writing only:

> "Chicago broke my continuity. This is permissible in life but not in writing. So I leave Chicago out, because it is off the line, out of drawing. In my travels, it was pleasant and good; in writing, it would only contribute to a disunity."

Rounding the western shore of the expansive and picturesque San Pablo Bay led to an open mix of farms and marshland at the southernmost end of Sonoma and Napa Counties in the North Coast wine region. This run along the bay's northern rim eventually narrowed to a more promising two-lane track – even though its charms were soon lost to heavy traffic and an overly sluggish pace (only made worse by glowing brake lights as far as the eye could see). Although a more relaxed drive is perfectly acceptable along a densely wooded trail or over a lonely mountain pass, it held no appeal in this mostly uninspired, rush-hour-like setting.

Several miles later, following that submission to the eight-lane I-80 (a nearly 3000-mile interstate that runs from San Francisco to New Jersey), a diagonal cut northeast across Solano County offered a reprieve both in speed and scenery. The steeply rolling hills and rich grasslands of Lynch Canyon – an open space preserve laced with hiking, biking and horse trails – momentarily softened the highway's starkness while the valley further east threaded the interstate nicely between the southern end of the Vaca Mountains and the Montezuma Hills to my right. Signs for Lake Berryessa and Lagoon Valley reignited thoughts of finding a more visually appealing route, but my GPS seemed unwilling to assist. The pursuit of scenery over superhighway once again thwarted, I pressed on past the vast patchwork of produce, beef and fiber farms of Vacaville, Dixon and Davis – fair compensation under the circumstances. Crossing the upper panhandle of Yolo County and entering the oak-dotted Sacramento Valley, I avoided the city traffic to the west, crossed over a bend in the 400-mile Sacramento River (rising from the Klamath Mountains where my journey began) and found myself in the home-away-from-home stretch.

Although by design I was traveling alone among strangers – a unique opportunity offering an introspective separateness and an enjoyable freedom of rhythm – I was looking forward to the lightness of visiting with Scot and his wife Dorthy in their cozy white rancher along Sacramento's northern county line. Content to be off the road earlier than usual, I was greeted warmly upon my late-afternoon arrival. Their guest room was comfortable; with a large bed and a nice desk for writing, and it felt good just to be in their home and away from hotels and gas stations for a couple of days. I enjoyed the travel, of course. But this time of relative stillness, relaxation and reconnection with familiar faces (and a new one in Mick – the black Labrador retriever) was welcome and I settled in easily.

Soon after arriving, and with early evening suggesting cocktail time, Scot and I headed across town – actually across the railroad tracks into

Roseville in Placer County (named for a type of gold mining) – for some dinner and drinks and a lot of catching up. There's something very singular about sitting at a bar far from home, having a drink and some good conversation with an old friend – truly an extension of home. It's not very detached from the type of travel I was pursuing as both have a tendency to be easy, enjoyable and welcome. This casual reconnection and shared familiarity was a sort of therapeutic response to the solitude of the road… and perhaps a subconscious refueling of my mental gas tank as well. A line from an unrelated article I read in the quiet of my hotel room only two days after my visit with Scot could well be from the perspective of a traveler and to varying degrees seemed to apply to the pros and cons of that solitude: "A little bit of loneliness and isolation, a little bit of confusion… all the good stuff."

Continuing our conversation over dinner at a nearby table afforded us time for a few more memories and a few more rounds (*other* "good stuff") before calling it a night. While recounting the day's events in my journal before turning in later that evening, I was reminded of a message in a Rush song and made a brief entry about it:

> "Was great to catch up tonight – *'to pass an evening with a drink and a friend'* ("Time Stand Still"). So many lines speak well to how I'm trying to experience this drive… slow down, live in the moment, take it all in, observe, enjoy and feel as much as possible along the way. To *'see more of the people and the places that surround me now…'* So far, so good at trying to 'still time' for those mental snapshots (and these 'voluminous' notes). All in all… good food, good drink, good company, good day."

The morning sun, rising quickly in a mostly cloudless sky, held the promise of more picture-perfect weather as the day began to unfold. Returning to the neighborhood where I lived with Scot all those years ago and having lunch with him and his sister Heather at one of the restaurants he manages were enjoyable parts of a very loose itinerary that also included a long-awaited "tour" of his man cave and all the rock'n'roll (and sports, TV and movie) memorabilia within. Aside from the beautiful 1986 Rowe AMI jukebox in the family room, this extensive and notable collection of albums, pictures and various keepsakes from years of concerts, artist run-ins and other events (all well documented and referenced) spoke well to his passion for the music and artists of the 1960s, '70s and '80s and covered nearly all visible wall and shelf space. But the pièce de résistance and focal point of this collection – representing his favorite band – is perhaps best exemplified by a vintage, well-preserved and working 1980 Rolling Stones pinball machine.

In keeping with our shared interest in all this music, Scot made plans for us to see '80s band Missing Persons that night at a small venue in Downtown Sacramento – a thriving area just south of the American River and fewer than fifty miles west of the 1848 discovery of gold in its waters by James Marshall. Designated as California's capital city a few years after the eventual gold rush of 1849 (and well after San Jose, Vallejo and Benicia each held that title), it was bustling with activity, culture and eateries and we scanned only a few before settling in to the brick-walled and plank-floored atmosphere of the local Iron Horse Tavern. Our conversation – once again an easy flow of memories and moments as viewed through the lens of present age and circumstances – continued beneath the busy Saturday-night din as our contagiously cheerful server Katie took our dinner orders and dutifully kept us from... thirst.

Walking down a side street after dinner, we encountered Missing Persons singer Dale Bozzio with both her son and her manager. After a brief and pleasant exchange about their music and the music of the '80s in general, Dale agreeably posed for a picture with Scot – one that's sure to make the man-cave wall or record book – before continuing on to the venue. This was another moment not atypical of our respective "behind-the-scenes" practices at concerts even though it was the first such one experienced together. Proving an enjoyable bit of time travel – apropos of my visit – the show was followed by perhaps too much time at the rustic and barn-like R15 Bar next door. But having wisely taken a Lyft that evening (which included a surprisingly informed discussion about classic rock with our driver), under the late-night and "celebratory" circumstances, it served us very well for the (hazy) return ride home.

Reasons for a late night... reasons for a late morning

With our shared appreciation for both the finer details of music and those countless places of magic, I had hoped to extend my visit with Scot by having him ride shotgun for the next leg of my drive – a wandering exploration of the Bay Area. Unfortunately, his schedule didn't permit and the following morning I was off again on my solo trek toward the coast.

In contrast to Steinbeck's experience with Chicago, my out-of-the-way trek to Citrus Heights was both a well-placed break in my scenic driving and an enjoyable time of repose. Indeed it was "pleasant and good" – well worth some ink on these pages and hopefully not a disunity to the reader. What it lacked in "inspection of a countryside" it more than made up for by reinforcing the solid roots of a decades-long, cross-country friendship – its own type of scenic landscape where memories of good times reside. As Bob Seger sings in "Hollywood Nights"… *"See some old friends, good for the soul…"*

When life takes over and a handful of years (or more) tend to pass between visits with friends, any opportunity to raise a glass, break some bread and reconnect while there's still some sand left in the hourglass is best heeded. As English poet and author Samuel Butler once said, "Keep your friendships in repair."

SEVEN

Moving On to the Past

Nothing behind me, everything ahead of me, as is ever so on the road

~ Jack Kerouac

A somewhat disquieting and heavy scent of smoke permeated the late-morning air for several miles arouwnd the Sacramento River as my visit ended and the city gradually faded from view (the previous night out with Scot having hindered any attempt at an early rise). In a state where disastrous wildfires often rage (eight of its twenty worst have occurred in the past decade) and aided by similarly dry conditions, it seemed cause for concern – at least to this outsider. But I wondered if, to some extent, the locals knew what to truly worry about and either dismissed or had become desensitized to seemingly lesser threats.

With a breeze blowing in from the west, the scent began to dissipate just east of Davis. As my tolerance for the featureless I-80 reached its limit and the opening chords of Tom Petty and the Heartbreakers' 1977 song "American Girl" rang out in perfect synch, I decided to trade highway for byway – always in search of the road less traveled. Running at an increasingly widespread parallel this adjacent and dusty two-lane through wide-open produce farms and cattle ranches made the grade, bringing about an immediate change of pace and a renewed level of enjoyment as the distant Napa Valley drew ever closer.

At the edge of town across from a small, two-pump gas station a sign announced: "Next Fuel 32 Miles." This promising indication of some very welcome and solitary driving would be the perfect change of scenery – improved only by a merger with the Putah Creek to my left. A vague roadside warning – "Slide Area" – seemed open to interpretation as several miles of meandering track led deeper into the foothills of the Vaca Mountains. My route, as usual, anything but direct.

An alternating mix of lush groundcover and outwardly impenetrable woody thickets lined the shoulder of the road while an assortment of trees in full canopy – Oregon ash, cottonwood and valley oak, among others – dotted higher elevations of the golden hillsides. This area overlooking the 1023-foot-wide Monticello Dam was an intersection of three county lines – southwest Yolo, northwest Solano and the eastern border of Napa. Crossing the Putah Creek Bridge to a winding track along the water's edge allowed me to pass through all three counties in a matter of minutes. Enormous shale outcroppings to my left appeared pale gray in the reflected sunlight and marked the northern edge of the Putah Creek State Wildlife Reserve (a sign indicating "Rock Slide Area" was more revealing this time). This nearly 700-acre protected area of both gently sloping and steep hillsides bordered the dammed and pristine blue waters to my right, which I soon discovered were part of the southernmost branch of the previously elusive Lake Berryessa – the largest lake in Napa County.

This beautifully forested and mostly isolated drive along Highway

128 proved every bit as enjoyable as anticipated. A fairly straight and mountainous climb soon led to a more gratifying, twisting and descending run as gravity pulled me toward the small, quiet and briefly mystifying farming community of Capell Valley. A vacant motel-restaurant and boarded-up gas station belied the surrounding and seemingly well-tended farms. But without a soul in sight, my first impression was one of desertion. In his book, *The American West as Living Space,* American novelist and historian Wallace Stegner wrote about the sometimes-conflicting impression of small, remote and sparsely populated towns:

> "They look at once lost and self-sufficient, scruffy and indispensable. A road leads in out of wide emptiness, threads a fringe of service stations, taverns, and a motel or two, widens to a couple of blocks of commercial buildings, some still false-fronted, with glimpses of side streets and green lawns, narrows to another strip of automotive roadside, and disappears into more wide emptiness."

Although Capell Valley seemed unlikely to have more than one of anything, this perceived lack of pizazz held its own distinct appeal. While my intended route south called for a left at the fork in the road, curiosity had me veering right where I stopped to stretch my legs in the motel's understandably unused parking lot. Theroux further described the somewhat somber attraction to this type of emptiness in *Deep South*:

> "… yet another reason why travel in these parts was such a melancholy pleasure… the sunny day, the bleakness of the countryside, the old bungalow on the narrow road, no other house nearby, the smell of the muddy fields penetrating the room – and that other thing, a great and overwhelming sadness that I felt but couldn't fathom."

An old, faded and weather-beaten sign – "Moskowite Lodge" (named for a longtime local rancher, entrepreneur and civic leader who passed away during this writing) – included "Restaurant, Cocktails, Groceries and Fishing Supplies" among its one-time offerings. And while a heavy peacefulness pervaded all this absence, it quickly lightened when a few modest hints of life appeared around a hillside bend; a small mobile-home park, a boat-and-trailer storage yard and a farm with grazing horses and heavy equipment. It looked as though little more was necessary or even belonged in this fittingly rural setting. Being nestled in a valley and closed off to any possible growth that may be offered by more open land keeps such towns smaller. But when I returned the way I came and discovered the small Moss Creek Winery set back off a side road against what I later learned were its Cabernet Sauvignon vineyards, it seemed to complete the scene – offering further proof that I had somewhat misread this little pocket of the Napa Valley.

The road that slipped past the trees as I drove away began to feel a bit like a Grand Prix course – or what I imagined one to be. Zigging and zagging along a winding two-lane blacktop with blind curves, guardrails and alternating stretches of sun and shade – occasionally at more-than-sensible speeds – kept me extremely focused. Where the leafy tunnels left off, wide-open skies took over and for the next thirty or forty miles this leg of my journey was pure and simple enjoyment.

Only a week after passing through, however, my earlier cause for concern was realized by the residents of Capell Valley when, at the hand of an arsonist, a wildfire ravaged more than one-hundred acres of local forested land. Most residences and businesses were protected by the open farmland east of the highway and, as a result, the valley was spared the structural damage that typically occurs in more densely wooded areas. Once again, the timing of my drive was mere happenstance. And upon learning of the fire some weeks later I felt fortunate to have passed through beforehand... to have avoided any backtracking or road closures and to have seen this rustic and remote part of the Napa Valley in all its uncharred and uncomplicated perfection.

Billed as the "Summer of Love" (ironically as the Vietnam War was escalating), 1967 came to represent a shift in the landscape of American culture and an awakening of sorts that fired up the imaginations of countless young people, inspiring many to reassess the lives and ideas into which they were respectively born and raised. This movement, simultaneously political, sexual, musical, drug-related and otherwise alternative, called for its disciples to "turn on, tune in and drop out." It was the year when Jann Wenner first published *Rolling Stone* magazine (in San Francisco), when the Beatles released *Sgt. Pepper's Lonely Hearts Club Band* and when "Brown Eyed Girl" (Van Morrison), "Happy Together" (The Turtles) and "Get Together" (The Youngbloods' version) spoke to times of yearning and cautionary optimism... *"Come on people now, smile on your brother, everybody get together, try to love one another right now..."*

When a "Human Be-In" and another hit song ("San Francisco" - Scott McKenzie) proved successful at stirring the masses to convene in one place (preferably with some flowers in their hair), the "City by the Bay" – San Francisco – quickly became defined as "ground zero of the hippie movement," according to the late journalist and *CBS Evening News* anchor Harry Reasoner. It was a counterculture that is now, in many surviving ways, simply the culture. And so, on this 50th anniversary of that seminal summer, a visit was a must.

Finishing out my run through the Napa Valley and rolling along the eastern shore of San Pablo Bay, I passed the waterfront city and former state capital of Vallejo, crossed the Carquinez Strait and hugged the bay shore all the way to the Richmond-San Rafael Bridge. With a rising and falling span of nearly six miles, it was considered the world's second-longest bridge (behind the San Francisco-Oakland Bay Bridge to the south - 1936) and the longest continuous steel span when completed in 1956. Carrying

Interstate 580 across the northern end of San Francisco Bay it delivered me directly into the small community of San Quentin, its renowned and namesake prison visible upon crossing and sitting in sharp relief to the idyllic waterfront setting to the south. The shadow of Mount Tamalpais at the southern tip of the North Coast Ranges was likely, to those on the inside, a glaring reminder of all the beauty and freedom that lay just beyond those demanding gates. As Petty alluded to earlier on my drive...
"God, it's so painful when something that's so close, is still so far out of reach..."

Continuing south along The 101 adjacent to Sausalito and on through the Robin Williams Tunnel (the late actor-comedian formerly from nearby Paradise Cay), my exit was met with an immediate view of that other famous Marin County landmark and coda to the coast... the Golden Gate Bridge. At 8,981 feet long and 746 feet tall it, too, was the longest and tallest suspension bridge in the world at the time of its 1937 opening. The unmistakable (and purposeful) radiance of the aligned north and south towers stood tall against the distant backdrop of the Santa Cruz Mountains as the waters of the Pacific flowed freely beneath. And although the Navy originally requested the bridge be painted black with yellow stripes, the international orange primer remained its permanent color – proving highly visible through the daily blanket of fog across the bay and becoming one of its most distinguishable characteristics to this day.

As I crossed both bridge and bay for the first time in more than two decades, the San Francisco skyline came clearly into view bringing with it memories of previous visits. In Jack Kerouac's 1957 novel *On The Road* he vividly describes his first impression of this city upon arrival with some friends in the late '40s:

> "It seemed like a matter of minutes when we began rolling
> in the foothills before Oakland and suddenly reached a
> height and saw stretched out ahead of us the fabulous
> white city of San Francisco on her eleven mystic hills with
> the blue Pacific and its advancing wall of potato-patch fog

beyond, and smoke and goldenness of the late afternoon of time."

The sight of an island to the east with a long military and prison history, a downtown high-rise building pointing uniquely skyward and an art deco tower sitting high atop a former military observation deck were all clear indications of my arrival in this breakpoint coastal city. Framed by water – both ocean and bay – and replete with distant and captivating views, a sense of openness prevailed as Alcatraz Island (1934), the Transamerica Pyramid (1972 - the tallest local building for forty-five years until this very summer) and Coit Tower (1933) each played their part. Even the eventual sight and sound of active cable cars slowly shuttling riders through the seemingly vertical streets further reminded me that I was, indeed, back in the city (and county) of San Francisco.

At Hyde & Beach - Alcatraz and Angel Island in the distance

As with most city travel, however, there was a keen awareness that any truly scenic driving would be on hold for the duration of my visit. There's a certain beauty in all the architecture, of course. But the cool detachment of concrete and metal held little appeal for me this time around. Further, the cold reality of souls on the street in their tattered clothing making the best of ramshackle dwellings and hard times was disheartening to say the least. Regardless of the gaze we use individually – critical, fearful, compassionate – the circumstances remain harsh and sobering. While reviewing my many notes about this visit, a lyric from "The Camera Eye" by Rush came to mind and seemed an apt summation of what I was thinking at the time… *"I feel the sense of possibilities, I feel the wrench of hard realities, the focus is sharp in the city…"*

Making my way along the flat terrain of the waterfront, I eased slowly through the Marina District and past the renowned Fisherman's Wharf and Pier 39. Unsure if my arrival on a Sunday was simply unfortunate timing, I became immediately curious as to whether the intense congestion had become the new norm. Both the road and sidewalk squirmed with foot traffic; the area seemingly so dense with tourists that all attention had to be devoted to not hitting anyone… or to not being hit. Even later at Russian Hill my attempt to escape down the renowned one-block, red-brick section of Lombard Street was thwarted by police as two female officers waved all traffic past. This so-called "crookedest street in the world" with its famously steep grade, eight hairpin turns and bow-windowed rowhouses was a major tourist attraction. I would guess any respite from the deluge of traffic and gawkers – reportedly upward of 2600 cars and trucks daily – was likely appreciated by its residents. Further along the Embarcadero's palm-tree-lined waterfront, past more piers of historic prominence and present reclamation and just beyond the Ferry Building (1898), the congestion eased considerably. As the Bay Bridge came more clearly into view, I turned inland again toward the heart of the city and on to more personally interesting sights.

The streets and sidewalks of San Francisco

It was once again the music-related venues and landmarks – both here and gone – that were my true fascination and, as such, among some of the stops on my jaunt through town. The legendary and still-active Fillmore concert hall (1912), the site of the long-gone Winterland Ballroom (1928) and Wally Heider Recording (1969) – now Hyde Street Studios – are all musically rich and historic places that helped give rise to San Francisco's burgeoning reputation as a musical mecca. Some of the biggest bands of the '60s and '70s... The Grateful Dead, Jefferson Airplane and Journey, among others, came to be in this town that's so widely considered the epicenter of the "hippie movement." Live recordings by Peter Frampton, Jimi Hendrix, Santana and more were forever captured from the stages of these and other well-regarded local venues. Initially shared with the world on vinyl, their chart successes (as well as the realization of the nearby Monterey Pop Festival) further reinforced the Bay Area's standing as a favorable artistic enclave. Even the now-famous intersection just east of Golden Gate Park – the corner of Haight and Ashbury streets – became synonymous with the music and hedonistic happenings of its surroundings and time.

Named for two influential local businessmen from the 1800s – Henry

Haight and Munroe Ashbury (both of whom helped create the park) – this area known locally as "The Haight" was not particularly busy on this late afternoon offering a welcome opportunity for me to walk its streets "far from the madding crowd" along the waterfront. As both the creative center of San Francisco and perhaps the countercultural center of the world in 1967, it often holds the most recounted memories by those who were there at the time (in spite of the old line: "If you remember the '60s, you weren't really there."). Former president of Atlantic Records and American political advocate, Danny Goldberg, wrote about the era's "collection of energies" that seemed to overlap and harmonize with one another in his 2017 book *In Search of the Lost Chord: 1967 and the Hippie Idea:*

> "I never felt aligned with just one faction but with the ephemeral collective vibe that permeated the culture. Time was so compressed that many of the signature events of 1967 happened within hours or days of each other. Often they were intertwined. My fascination is with the whole, not merely its parts. However, if I could time travel back to 1967, there is no question that I would begin in the Haight-Ashbury section of San Francisco."

Since its days as "a conglomerate of dunes, farms and ranches" in the early 1800s, it has weathered many economic climates taking turns as a wealthy residential settlement (1890s), a town in decline (1950s) and a culturally accelerated community (1960s) – the period of time which seems to have most endured, albeit in the form of a touristy flashback. Despite the visual alliteration of larger-than-life murals of Jerry, Jim, Janis, Jimi and George (Garcia, Morrison, Joplin, Hendrix and Harrison respectively) looming high above the sidewalks as well as all manner of tie-dyed garb and psychedelia being offered by various uniquely adorned boutiques and head shops (some mirroring the look of the '60s), I found its legendary streets to be relatively unassuming, although quite colorful and musical.

Sounds of that bygone era wafted through the air like so much incense and marijuana by way of storefront sound systems or sidewalk performers. Indeed a perfect backdrop and soundtrack to my visit.

As I returned to my Jeep under full, late-day sun, my thoughts drifted back to the song that helped inspire a movement five decades earlier; its tune staying with me as I broke free of the concrete and metal and made my way west toward the Pacific by way of Golden Gate Park... *"If you're going to San Francisco, be sure to wear some flowers in your hair..."*

English writer and poet Rudyard Kipling once said, "San Francisco has only one drawback – 'tis hard to leave." But I found no figurative or literal certainty in that statement as my time there, though enjoyable enough, was...well, enough. And the transition back to scenic from city was both easy and immediate.

Only three miles long, Golden Gate Park was San Francisco's answer to New York's Central Park when plans were conceived for it in the late 1860s. More than 150 years later the patchwork of hills, lakes, meadows, gardens and woodlands has long since come into its own as a quick escape to some semblance of wilderness in the midst of the surrounding city. And my drive – from its entrance just west of The Haight along its relaxed curves and all the way out to the windswept sands of the Pacific – was almost clichéd in its tranquility. This visually pleasing run through Monterey pines, cypress, redwoods and native coast live oaks was a welcome segue back to a more appealing, natural and coastal landscape.

Exiting the park, I continued south for several sea-level miles along the Great Highway where the waves lapping at the shore of Ocean Beach lulled me into a peaceful bliss and reminded me why we are so drawn to water – easily as much about scenery as science. In a 2010 study at Plymouth University in the United Kingdom, pictures of various natural and urban environments were rated by forty individuals. They associated positive moods, preference and perceived health restorativeness to any images containing water – whether in a natural landscape or urban setting – as opposed to those images without water shown. The indication is that our innate relationship to water may contribute to our health and well-being beyond the obvious necessity and may be more influential in our lives than we casually realize. We certainly experience moments of inspiration when seeing bodies of water, tend to feel a sense of calm when hearing a cascading stream and often want to be near or in it as evident by so many real estate transactions and vacation destinations. It even plays out in myriad ways in so much of our music, art, literature and poetry. American scientist and marine biologist Dr. Wallace J. Nichols wrote about water's contribution to our state of being and the value of periodically disconnecting in *Blue Mind*:

> "Water's amazing influence does not mean that it displaces other concerted efforts to reach a mindful state; rather, it adds to, enhances, and expands. In an age when we're anchored by stress, technology, exile from the natural world, professional suffocation, personal anxiety, and hospital bills, and at a loss for true privacy, casting off is wonderful. I believe that oceans, lakes, rivers, pools, even fountains can irresistibly affect our minds. And there are logical explanations for our tendency to go to the water's edge for some of the most significant moments of our lives."

The peaceful bliss of another shoreline drive

Ending at the western shore of a very still and tranquil-looking Lake Merced, the highway picked up at Skyline Boulevard, quickly crossed the San Mateo County line and temporarily reconnected me with the PCH just south of Pacifica Beach where it slowly climbed and disappeared into the woods. This welcome bit of two-lane was an extension of that relaxed coastal feel blanketed by greenery; the sun tangled in the trees. At the far end of this brief stand, the entrance to Devil's Slide tunnel cut through Pedro Mountain. This recently opened bypass to the steep and rocky headland trail of the same name took me past eroded cliffs just above the highway; the sharp truncations of vegetated areas visible from below. Signs posting modest speed limits and warnings of "Rock Slide Area" along this winding track overlooking the Pacific were replaced by less cautious speeds and suggestions to "Share the Road" with bicyclists as it straightened out and leveled off on descent. These occasionally abrupt variations in terrain and scenery were all part of the magic of nature and precisely what I hoped to see when I set out on this journey. Some of it to plan, most left to chance, all endlessly captivating.

Several miles later, past a long stretch of farmlands and small neighboring communities, I opted off the PCH once again for more inland travel among a canopy of dense leafy trees. Turning from the coast at Half

Moon Bay – a name inspired by the shape of its coastal inlet – four lanes almost immediately narrowed to two and the road out of town became more inviting. Curling its way back up to Skyline Boulevard and hugging the ridged spine of the Santa Cruz Mountains, it was another visit to one of my views – this one from Sausalito earlier in the day. With the tempting prospect of being swallowed up by trees, the twisting and turning north-south line that intermittently crossed in and out of Santa Clara and Santa Cruz counties was one of those few routes specifically considered during the planning stages of this trip – and it delivered as I had hoped. Until it no longer could.

Ascending from the bay to more than 3800 feet above sea level was a more-than-worthwhile detour from the coast. While a lacework shade filtered through the redwoods offering a unique and agreeable intimacy, occasional hillside exposures allowed for landscape views both far and wide; sweeping away in broad strokes to the horizon as the deep blue sky faded to white at the fringes. Unfortunately, the panoramic shots I had taken from these various vista points were foreshortened and a far cry from doing those views any justice. An immediate realization (ah, digital technology), it prompted the welcome task of staying a while longer each time in an effort to capture the views and the overall sense of place more vividly in my mind. One of my brief but forward-looking journal notes from this high-altitude run seems to sum it up well:

> "In the telling, maybe add a twist on the old cliché that 'you had to be there' – because unique and amazing views!"

A mostly lonely road punctuated at times by signs of current and former life, it was an extraordinary example of another path typically driven on only by locals. A dilapidated and abandoned roadside cabin once someone's home; now moldering in the coastal weather. A cluster of mailboxes at the end of a single driveway; the houses tucked away somewhere among the trees. Even a restaurant suggestive of a little red cabin nestled in the woods and aptly named The Mountain House. All of these dotted the way in this beautifully simple setting that was to lead to my next planned stop – the beach-and-boardwalk town of Santa Cruz. But those rains back in February apparently had lingering effects and now it seemed the road had other plans for me.

Although stops along the way are always part of a road trip and self-imposed detours or "longcuts" only add to the experience, signs forcing my hand in a singular alternate direction always give me pause. Perhaps it's the loss of control – the impression that someone or something else is now dictating some part of my journey. Of course, I'm always aware that an element of adventure could apply and the possibility was that it may very well turn out fine. But at the outset it's not very welcome. In *When the Road Ends* from Peart's 2011 anthology *Far and Away: A Prize Every Time,* he relates a similar frame of mind about road closures that have no immediately available detours and how the dreaded backtracking is always a last resort:

> "Unless a particular road ends at the ocean, say, or at a high-mountain retreat, it is an uncomfortable feeling to have your way suddenly blocked… my whole being recoils at the thought of going back the way I have come, and I'll do anything I can to avoid it."

Aside from the usual weather-beaten erosion along the coastal cliffs and the roadside signs warning of rock slides, until now there had been no ostensible reason for concern. No indication of any impassable conditions (other than that halted effort at Scenic Drive back in Trinidad). Even occasional roadwork being done during the past few days to repair residual damage from harsh winters and extreme thaws along various mountain passes only narrowed those roads to alternating stretches of one-way traffic.

And with flaggers controlling the flow even the considerable wait times were a "traffic jam" admittedly much easier to take in this wooded setting. But there it was – "Road Closed - Local Traffic Only." A quick Google search of current road conditions filled in the gaps, as it were. With a large section of Skyline Boulevard completely washed away several miles south near Los Gatos, it was suddenly time to change course as I sat at this vista-point intersection atop the Santa Cruz Mountains.

With a large green sign pointing me west at the county line along Highway 9 and another smaller one letting me know what was off to the east, I pulled out my trusty map, spread it open on the hood and considered the options. Running my finger along a thin gray line (an "undivided, two-way through road," according to the map's legend), I traced a detour south as it gradually snaked its way through a forested landscape toward Big Basin Redwoods State Park (California's oldest - 1902) and Boulder Creek. This fairly direct run terminating in Santa Cruz at the northern end of Monterey Bay was initially very inviting as two lanes through the mountains always held the promise of good driving. But it was a different thin gray line that zig-zagged east and down into Saratoga where a divided four-lane cut through town and connected with another encouraging run – Highway 17 (the Santa Cruz Highway). The road that sparked my interest in all this scenic driving nearly thirty-five years earlier. Although my waypoint destination was in the other direction, plans to avoid the shortest course and to once again rendezvous with that memorable old highway had me rerouting my journey south... by heading east.

A thick stand of trees continued to blanket the road through a series of winding stretches; many narrow and calling for slower speeds than anticipated. Occasional signs with images of bikes and more reminders to "Share the Road" made me curious about who would want to ride these somewhat unpredictable and descending passes so vulnerably – even though I clearly understood it from a scenic perspective. Similar to others I had seen – "Bikes Can Use Lanes Thru Mountains" and (with a large image of a bike) "May Use Full Lane" – these signs were an obvious nod to the prevalence of cycling in the area. This was something I experienced firsthand coming up behind a large group of riders in a redwood grove just north of Fort Bragg. It was actually interesting to witness; the tandem approach, the fluid and unrelenting pedaling, the leaning in along a series of blind and downhill curves all while maintaining a fairly impressive (and gravity-assisted) pace. And as I was rarely interested in "flying" through any of this landscape anyway, the unavoidably reduced approach (a true speed "limit") was of no bother.

A gradual thinning of the trees at lower elevations coincided with an increase in homes, shops and other signs of life as the road threaded the valley into Saratoga; an upscale residential community tucked away in the foothills. A slow and easy drive through an array of neatly aligned storefronts and well-manicured properties along the main thoroughfare seemed to speak well to its website claim offering "a high quality of life to its residents and a chance to escape the hustle of Silicon Valley." This reminded me of an article I previously read about Silicon Valley residents leaving for the more grim reasons of a crumbling infrastructure, worsening crime and increased traffic (among other concerns and statewide issues that continue to be reflected in its more recent depopulation). This peacefulness in Saratoga was an apropos segue into Monte Sereno ("serene hill") – where Steinbeck lived when he wrote *The Grapes of Wrath* – which led further on to Los Gatos ("the cats") where my anticipated reconnection with Highway 17 south was finally realized.

This stretch of road has a long history of calling for courage and skill from those who traverse its many twists, turns and grades – dating back to the time of four- and six-horse stagecoaches and the gold rush of 1849. Back to a time before the South Coast Railroad came through (1880) and before widespread use of asphalt pavement made for quicker and more comfortable travel. And while that earlier experience on "17" was only as a passenger, I was immediately aware of the inherent danger in most of its nearly twenty-seven miles. Although I viewed that danger (almost exclusively) as exciting at the time.

Several easy and relatively straight miles later, a bright yellow sign "promised" me at least a modicum of something I had been hoping would appear sooner than later: "Winding Road Next 8 Miles." Not that I hadn't already experienced some memorable roads along the way, but this had been a long-awaited return. As to my ongoing fascination with visiting my view across some great expanse ahead, I was now visiting a memory from my fairly distant past and hoping it would measure up. Songs on the radio had amounted to little more than white noise for a few miles as I crossed into Santa Cruz County along the 1800-foot summit at Patchen Pass. Truly soaking up the details of those rolling and ascending foothills proved a bit of a challenge as they slipped past in a blur of vivid green flora and bright blue skies. But when Deep Purple's "Knocking at Your Back Door" began cranking along in its modest 4/4 time, both the tempo and delivery somehow seemed to match the overall mood of the road and the sign began to make good on its promise.

Descending runs fueled by gravity tested my brakes as hairpin curves – like asphalt ribbons against the mountain – narrowed my concentration; prohibiting any opportunity to more fully take in views of distant valleys or ravines. And while some winding highland runs will ebb and flow with the terrain, this particular four-lane seemed to be an uninterrupted speedway requiring hands on the wheel at "ten and two" and an unwavering focus on whatever may lie around each bend. Unlike most other courses on my journey, this one was not chosen for its scenic merits (though not for a lack of them). But rather for all that's been described here – mile after mile of fast-paced, adrenaline-surging twists, turns, climbs and descents. Just as the element of excitement was recalled from years past (even though the road seemed new to me after all this time), its corresponding hazards were not lost on me in the present.

As the road began to straighten out and level off, I fell into a more relaxed rhythm as my time on Highway 17 neared its end. Wending my way south through Scotts Valley along the upland slope of the Santa Cruz Mountains eventually brought me straight down into Santa Cruz where the sea air was noticeably fragrant and cooler. Twilight cast its gauzy half-light across the sky as a bright full moon – already hanging low in the east – reminded me that my first order of business was to find a bed for the night. Another nicely-appointed room at the local Best Western Inn just east of the San Lorenzo River fit the bill and I settled in quickly by tossing my bag on the bed, shaking off the proverbial road dust and grabbing my journal. Soon enough, I was headed out for a walk around town (always welcome after so many hours of driving) in an effort to accomplish my second order of business... a late dinner.

Caught between the moon and Santa Cruz

Several blocks later I was sitting at a quiet and candlelit corner table in the unpretentious elegance of the Hindquarter Bar & Grill. The brick-and-wood interior with burgundy accents, soft lighting and the mouthwatering aroma of a steakhouse was relaxing and offered a perfectly subdued atmosphere so necessary for my third and final order of business for the evening... catching up on my notes. After taking my order and bringing my drink, the very pleasant Laurie left me alone to ruminate on my day, to slowly sip my "reward" and – after allowing mind and body to truly feel the effects of being contentedly motionless – to pull out my pen and begin capturing it all in words.

EIGHT
Monterey Bay Day

The combination of time and place was pleasant... and I loved it

~ Neil Peart

Signs at town entrances throughout the country are many and varied ranging from the straightforward to the expressive – the latter typically an effort at either heartwarming or humorous as discovered in more than a few communities along my route. But the large carved-wood sign that received visitors into this beach resort on the northern end of Monterey Bay was both friendly ("Welcome to Santa Cruz") and interesting displaying the names of six "Sister Cities" (one of which no longer applies). Familiar with little more than the term and noting the exotic-sounding diversity of locales that spanned the globe from Jinotepe, Nicaragua and Puerto La

Cruz, Venezuela to Sestri Levante, Italy; Alushta, Ukraine and Shingu, Japan, I made a note to follow up.

It seems that the concept, sometimes referred to as Twin Towns, has been around for centuries – the earliest known example being the pairing of Paderborn, Germany and Le Mans, France in 836. And although more modern efforts were conceived after World War II in an effort to encourage peace and reconciliation among former adversaries, the first such agreement in the United States occurred under same-name circumstances when the (Lucas) county seat of Toledo, Ohio and central Spain's ancient city of Toledo paired up in 1931 (well before the 1956 founding of Sister Cities International by President Eisenhower).

Essentially a voluntary agreement between towns, states and even countries, the idea was to create mutual benefits both casual and professional. From simple cultural understandings and friendships to trade agreements and business partnerships, the program has resulted in myriad connections worldwide to include more than 140 countries. Occasionally extending well beyond one or two cities (as with Santa Cruz), these sisterhoods may also share social or geographic characteristics as part of their connection with one another. Perhaps the most apparent parallel between Santa Cruz and its sister cities is that nearly all are coastal towns with economies that benefit from their proximity to the water (the landlocked Jinotepe being the sole exception). Inspired by this overall theme, I reviewed my notes and did a bit of research to discover that at least twenty-three cities or towns I had either visited or passed through on this journey had at least one sister city (many with more) – the program far more established and pervasive than I would have previously guessed.

Noted simply in my journal as "the first time so far," unusually overcast skies greeted me the following morning as I set out for the renowned and historic Santa Cruz Beach Boardwalk – home to the oldest surviving amusement park in the state (1907) and a California Historical Landmark

(1990). Not allowing the weather to equally diminish my outlook, I parked and made my way to the fittingly cheerful entrance (complete with an enormous sign and large faux beach balls) just as the clouds slowly began to dissipate and the seasonable temperatures started to feel even more so. This early arrival found the boardwalk and all its attractions empty and strangely quiet. Even the waves splashing along the shoreline too far off to contribute their usual music. The stilled Sky Glider hung readily and high above as the wooden Giant Dipper roller coaster and Looff Carousel – both National Historic Landmarks (1987) – seemed quietly inconsequential without the sunny jubilance of their respective riders. As with the road, however, there was a certain peacefulness in having the boards all to myself and walking them again evoked memories of the last time Highway 17 brought me here so many years ago.

The world seems to reward those who rise early. And as I stepped onto the sand and kicked off my flip-flops, the arriving sunlight warmed my shoulders and began to dance across the water from the east causing it to glisten in an almost clichéd way – truly like diamonds along the shore. As two surfers in wetsuits drifted together in the calm shallows, a small fishing boat bobbed in the distance and a mist of blues and whites on the horizon fused water with sky. The beach, nearly deserted at this hour, was decidedly quiet as I walked from the Santa Cruz Wharf (the longest on the West Coast) to the Breakwater Walton Lighthouse (2001) at the tip of Seabright State Beach. It was an ideal way to begin the day; a more tangibly scenic course of relative stillness with bare feet deep in the warm sand followed by a walk along the cool water and some time in the sun. As easy to take as it was difficult to leave. But as I made my way from sand to street a few hours later Emerson's words echoed once again in the back of my mind becoming a commanding mantra for the rest of my trip – "demand a horizon." Although many stops along the way were sure to mesmerize, the mindset of always carrying on to somewhere else remained… *"What next?"*

One of many rewards for an early rise

A row of towering California fan palms along the mouth of the San Lorenzo River seemed to mark the way forward offering a fitting exit as I hugged the coast out of town. Wending my way past beautiful views of marinas, lagoons and lakes, I looked forward to visiting another place from my past. Even though this was a fairly direct and even sea-level run, it repeatedly alternated in and out of being a tsunami hazard zone – the residential areas apparently the designated safe spots. Signs once again pointed to the prevalence of cycling along the coast and politely urged drivers to "Be Courteous" and "Share the Road." The mix of ranch-style residential neighborhoods and long stretches of wide-open ocean views made for an agreeably slow and easy ramble all the way to the quaint seaside village of Capitola.

Following the fan palms

As the oldest coastal resort town in California (1874) there was a certain history here and its noted activities, arts and culture spoke well to that. But my plans for visiting were far less refined; a simple midday break from the road. An opportunity to briefly return to a place that held some fond memories for me and, not least, to grab a bite to eat (with a view, of course).

A stroll along the bayfront shops and restaurants of the bustling Esplanade – an area known as The Village – brought me to a cleverly named eatery and watering hole called The Sand Bar; an effortlessly casual "joint" overlooking Capitola Beach and the shallow waters of Soquel Creek. With the sky showing no further hint of its early morning gray and the temperature hovering comfortably in the mid-seventies, I took a seat on the deck where, after taking my order, my waitress Sarah nonchalantly shared that she "could look across that water all day."

Indeed the background was enhanced considerably by the colorful view of the well-known and remarkable Venetian Court condominiums along the beach. Completed in 1925 along with the architecturally consistent hotel just beyond, they were intended to bring the allure of Venice, Italy

113

to Capitola. Serving the city well, they've been listed on the National Register of Historic Places since 1987 and have been a primary focal point of the town – actually its classic postcard representation – for more than ninety years.

A stunning view - even in black & white

A decorative arcing sea wall adorned with tiles created by residents extended nearly 700 feet along the Esplanade to the water's edge. It was here where I spent my remaining time in Capitola – feet up just reading, relaxing and being in the moment (and the sun). Similar to what others were doing all around me it seemed to define this beachy little enclave. As I looked across Monterey Bay to its namesake city that bounds it in the distance – beyond which rises yet another inviting mountain range – I considered my next planned stop. Although less scenic in a natural sense it would be a worthy indulgence; a brief glimpse into some of the rich agricultural and literary landscape along the coast.

California can lay claim to a number of prolific and celebrated authors either by birth (Jack London, Robert Frost, Joan Didion) or written word (John Muir, Jack Kerouac). But by one measure or another one name always seems to rise to the top (with the city of Salinas often mentioned in the same breath) – John Steinbeck. As a personally favored writer for many years and a renowned progeny who immortalized his hometown in prose, a visit immediately became part of the plan. It was another opportunity to be in that place where something of note resonated so widely and personally. To be where many of his words and stories were written... and to walk some of the very streets that inspired them.

After a fairly straight and forested run just south of Capitola, an expanse of farmlands opened up on the outskirts of Watsonville and the view suddenly became far and wide. The Gabilan Ranges ("sparrow hawk") to the east and the Santa Lucia Mountains to the west both stood in faint profile against a distant sky, offering the only discernable texture to this otherwise flat and comparatively uninspired setting. But as with earlier drives through Arcata, Eureka and Ferndale, there was a peacefulness to all this open space; the patchwork fields appealing in their own right. Crossing the narrow Pajaro River ("bird") – which doubles as the twisting Monterey County line – I continued south through more big-sky country before opting off the highway at the small don't-blink-or-you'll-miss-it settlement of Castroville – "The Artichoke Center of the World," according to its large entrance sign. But I was no sooner in than out of that town and passing sprawling farmsteads that sporadically dotted several miles of rural two-lane pavement. Running parallel to the empty tracks of the Union Pacific Railroad, I continued on as Salinas ("salt works") and those mountains in the distance came more clearly into view.

As a prelude to this telling, I'm reminded of Steinbeck's words in a letter to his editor, Pascal Covici, while writing his 1952 novel *East of Eden*. Although not intended for publication, the letter was included with many others in *Journal of a Novel: The East of Eden Letters* published in 1968, one year after Steinbeck's death:

> "I want to describe the Salinas Valley in detail but in
> sparse detail so that there can be a real feeling of it. It

should be sights and sounds, smells and colors but put
down with simplicity..."

Sitting at the head of the long and narrow valley between the Gabilans
and Santa Lucias, this well-known and fertile expanse – once the bottom
of a one-hundred-mile inlet from the sea – has roots that date back to
the mid-1800s. When irrigation techniques improved farming, fruit and
vegetable producers began setting up shop in Salinas and by the early 1920s
it became one of the most prosperous cities in the United States on the
harvest of lettuce, sugar beets, broccoli and strawberries. Despite eventual
recognition through Steinbeck's novels *Of Mice and Men*, *The Grapes of
Wrath* and *East of Eden*, among others, as well as further industrial growth
in the 1950s and '60s, for better or worse the Salinas Valley never became
a true tourist destination. Decaying buildings along Main Street in the late
'50s became an issue that lasted for nearly a decade before demolitions and
restorations began. But driving past the lush green produce fields that earned
Salinas its nickname – "The Salad Bowl of the World" – and strolling the
active sidewalks of the downtown area, I saw little evidence of a city once
diminished by indifference or neglect. Rather, a sense of vitality seemed to
prevail as tourists and residents alike, all popping in and out of various shops
and restaurants, appeared tuned in to its unique character and charm.

Part of that charm, situated in the heart of historic Oldtown Salinas,
was the National Steinbeck Center (1998). And stopping by for a visit was
one of the more inspiring reasons for my pass through town. But in an
effort to first absorb even more of the local sights and sounds, I parked
several blocks away and walked those old roads without hurry. Quiet
and shaded side streets soon led me to the somewhat livelier atmosphere
along Main Street where the din of conversation was commensurate with
increased foot traffic. Where hanging baskets overflowing with brightly
colored hydrangeas, impatiens and begonias hung, somewhat thirsty, from
streetlamps. And where American sweetgum trees lined the sidewalks,
their full and deep-green canopies offering intermittent shade to those of

us ambling about. The façade of the Fox California Theater (1921) with its towering vertical burgundy-and-gold sign, oversized marquee and stand-alone ticket booth immediately stood out as architecturally unique and historic; a throwback among the many surrounding restaurants, boutiques and coffee shops. And at the far end of this thoroughfare, only two blocks east of Steinbeck's turreted Victorian boyhood home (1897), stood the sleek and considerably more modern Steinbeck Center.

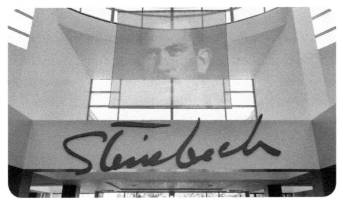

The poet of the people - the Steinbeck Center lobby

Appropriately, its impressive entrance was an invitation of sorts to another journey – this one through the historical, cultural and artistic landscape of Steinbeck's life and writings. Around each corner of the exhibit another time. In each room another story. A wide and detailed array of familiar characters imaginatively displayed against the backdrop of Salinas and other Central California settings (and beyond) takes the visitor into his books and onto the pages where the understanding and narrative are about shared experiences; those that bring us together both as community and country. Oversized maps of those well-documented and celebrated travels (*The Log from the Sea of Cortez* and *Travels with Charley*) as well as vintage pictures, memorabilia and several notable references are displayed on nearly every wall and surface, deepening the experience and allowing for a more intimate perspective. A fictional walk down the road in Monterey's Cannery Row (*Cannery Row*), a stroll along a warm Mexican beach (*The Forgotten Village* and *The Pearl*) and eventually a trip to the East Coast – where Steinbeck lived out his remaining days – each create a sense of being there… at that time… and among those people and their myriad circumstances. The effort by Steinbeck to recognize, understand and share elements of these conditions is evident in his writing. And this exhibit appeared to be a curator's extension of that effort – perhaps equally intended for those unfamiliar with his work.

In a finale befitting both Steinbeck and one of the few museums in the country devoted to a single author, there is a special area dedicated to an overview of his rich literary legacy. His twenty-seven published books (several adapted to stage or screen), election into the American Academy of Arts and Letters (1939), National Book Award and Pulitzer Prize for Fiction (*The Grapes of Wrath* - 1940) and Nobel Prize for Literature (1962) all certainly validate his place in the world of Western literature. Or at the very least they highlight his role in what he once referred to as the "strange and mystic business" of writing.

As those old roads took me slowly away from Salinas past the ghostly footsteps of its favored son, some of the images evoked by his words were enhanced by the reality of my travels. And looking around I realized that even though the houses, farms and fields were still the same as when I had arrived, I was now seeing them in a different light and through the lens of local history.

The Monterey Peninsula was a fairly straight run southwest through the Santa Lucias – the very range that "kept the valley from the sea," as Steinbeck wrote in *East of Eden*. These highlands have also more recently become home to a cool-climate winegrowing appellation of more than 6000 acres of Pinot Noir and Chardonnay grapes – a viticultural complement to the region's long history of vegetable and produce farming.

A sign proclaiming this pass as a "Scenic Route" was both encouraging and accurate as beautifully forested stretches and sunburnt hills ushered me all the way to the coast at Monterey. Situated at the southern end of the bay opposite Capitola and Santa Cruz, the city had a rich history; both real and imagined. And as I drove along the water past countless sailboats of all sizes peacefully moored in the marina at Fisherman's Wharf – like flashes of white against the blue; their masts high and bare – I briefly gave thought to where those factual and fictional lines overlapped before refocusing on the present.

Further along the waterfront was Cannery Row, legendary as the setting for Steinbeck's novels *Cannery Row* (1945) and *Sweet Thursday* (1954). Formerly Ocean View Drive, where several sardine canning companies expanded during World War II (and where most would close only a few years later when the sardines were depleted), it was officially renamed Cannery Row in 1958. This in spite of Steinbeck's rather vivid and less-than-flattering description of it in the opening passage of his book by the same name:

> "Cannery Row in Monterey, California is a poem, a stink, a grating noise, a quality of light, a tone, a nostalgia, a habit, a dream. Cannery Row is the gathered and scattered, tin and iron and rust and splintered wood, chipped pavement and weedy lots and junk heaps, sardine canneries of corrugated iron, honky tonks, restaurants and whore houses, and little crowded groceries, and laboratories and flophouses."

It is now quite different. Or perhaps merely an improved and far more contemporary version of its past with many of those descriptions left behind. Countless shops, restaurants and upscale hotels are now the dominant businesses; the last cannery having closed in 1973. But the "nostalgia" still survives in many ways. Not least at the corner of Cannery

Row and Prescott Avenue where the original 1917 Monterey Canning Company warehouse stands as the physical and focal center. Its large, two-story, red-painted and "corrugated iron" façade an unmistakable presence and photo attraction. Joining the throng of visitors strolling the sidewalks and side streets, I made an effort to take it all in – searching for hints of that seedy past amid its trendy present – before eventually continuing on.

A northwest trek along the coast ran parallel to the Monterey Bay Coastal Recreation Trail; formerly a stretch of abandoned railway once used by the Southern Pacific Railroad. Unobstructed views of the bay were buffered by a low-level, rocky coastline where occasional grassy areas supported large hardy and spiny mountain aloe bushes and other lush, green groundcover. This peaceful view accompanied me all the way out to the tip of the peninsula at Pacific Grove – so close to the water's edge (another tsunami hazard zone) that it allowed for the sound of crashing waves to be a soundtrack of sorts. But that same view was tinged with an element of melancholy as these were the same waters that took the life of American singer-songwriter John Denver just shy of his 54th birthday nearly twenty years before. Pulling into a sandy lot as an insistent onshore breeze helped cool the late afternoon, I walked to a small section of beach where a large stone sat hard against the water. Overlooking that beautiful yet fateful site where Denver's experimental plane went down, it displayed a memorial plaque dedicated nearly ten years after his passing – his image and the poignant chorus to his 1975 song "Windsong" inscribed beneath:

> *"... So welcome the wind and the wisdom she offers, follow her summons when she calls again, in your heart and your spirit let the breezes surround you, lift up your voice then and sing with the wind..."*

Striking views of the Pacific stretching away through shades of blue continued along Sunset Drive where unrelenting whitecaps broke against the jagged seawall spraying their saltwater mist and music into the air.

Signs warning of "Unexpected Life-Threatening Waves" and advising against "Climbing on Rocks, Swimming & Wading" seemed at odds with all this inherent beauty. And as I continued on in silence those ominous messages called to mind different lyrics from Denver's 1972 hit song "Rocky Mountain High." Somewhat prophetic they seemed to speak to the experimental nature of that final flight as well as his untimely and tragic end... *"And they say that he got crazy once, and he tried to touch the sun..."*

The greens of Pacific Grove Golf Links to the south and the white sands of Asilomar State Beach at Spanish Bay were visual echoes of the peacefulness all along this rich stretch of coastline. It seemed only fitting that they would lead to my pass through 17-Mile Drive in Pebble Beach. Although not some seldom-traveled back road or random nature path, this winding ramble (with an entrance fee) past stately golf courses, along vistas overlooking the bay and through sections of the Del Monte Forest brought with it a certain quiet and an inner stillness that seemed to lie just beneath. If there were any other cars on this drive, I hadn't noticed as the scenery and the various "points of interest" – to include some wandering along Old 17-Mile Drive – were more than enough to hold my attention.

There are no wrong turns at this intersection

Believing it was the entrance to Monterey Bay (originally Bahia de los Piños – "bay of the pines") and mistakenly setting it as their course, early mariners often crashed into the offshore rocks at Point Joe. As I walked along its vista-point overlook (plenty of other cars there) I saw and felt the effects of the wind and choppy waters of The Restless Sea as wave after wave washed over the rocks. A sign showing an old picture of "Joe's driftwood home" on the shore in 1895 noted inconclusively that "no one knows for sure if the point was named for Joe or if he was named after the point."

As the gentle rise and fall of the road continued south, curving around Fanshell Overlook and down to Cypress Point Lookout, it offered even more dramatic views of the Pacific (which never seemed to get old) eventually taking me to one of California's most enduring landmarks… The Lone Cypress. Considered one of the most photographed trees in North America, it's been overlooking the Monterey Peninsula from its wave-washed, granite perch for more than 250 years (stabilized with the assistance of partially hidden cables for the past seventy "in the hopes it will live to be 300," according to a nearby sign). Even though its species – the Monterey cypress (native only to this part of California) – typically reaches a height of eighty-five feet, consistently strong coastal winds and a limited root spread have contributed to its stunted growth (twenty-five feet) as well as its wide, flat-top canopy. But those unique characteristics and location have only enhanced its appeal – the Pebble Beach Company having wisely trademarked its image for use as their Heritage Logo since 1919.

Unfortunately, during this writing a severe winter storm snapped off a substantial section of the tree forever altering its appearance – but not likely the spirit of what it seems to represent. Although having been subjected to myriad natural and man-made threats in its time from storms and droughts to arson and spray painting, it still stands strong against all odds. An unlikely but rugged symbol of beauty, resolve and survival.

Soon after taking in this scene amid a small and scattered group of onlookers; many of whom seemed intent on capturing the perfect selfie with the Lone Cypress, I headed back to the Jeep, made a few notes and continued on past more well-manicured properties and carefully designed and flawless greens. But it was the occasional view across Stillwater Cove that offered the more natural backdrop of Point Lobos jutting out into Carmel Bay with the Santa Lucia Mountains rising just beyond. Their lure from afar was obvious and only improved upon closer inspection as awaiting me was an elevated and winding run clinging to the contours of that rugged coast. Taking that run turned out to be the only time on this trip that I deliberately disregarded my personal rule to avoid backtracking.

Keeping to the road less traveled had its own and obvious rewards. By presenting opportunities to pass through or visit small towns and villages along the way, it enhanced the overall experience considerably. Each community proved a complement to the many back roads and coastal runs that led to it adding both character and depth to varying degrees. Whether the quaint harbor town of Crescent City with its daybreak fog horn, the remote "Norman Rockwell-like" village of Nicasio or the much-celebrated and historic county seat of Salinas (shared with the world through Steinbeck's words), each town's unique setting and personality provided a perfect accent to my travels.

Carmel-by-the-Sea – a one-square-mile artist's haven on the bright blue water just south of 17-Mile Drive – was no exception to this trend. Contributing its own type of character, it retained an old-world charm through unique architecture and a handful of long-standing and appealingly unusual statutes. Walking among the boutiques, galleries and bookstores that make up Ocean Avenue (no T-shirt shops here) seemed a lesson in refined originality. Rustic storefronts with moss-covered cedar roofs abutted Chalet-style façades overflowing with bright pink bougainvillea and potato vine plants. Unusual home designs along the heavily shaded side streets continued this unique character trend and I immediately made some notes. It turns out many of the fairy-tale-inspired cottages, bungalows and storefronts date back to the 1920s. Similarly influenced and enchanting names such as Oceans End, Sea Haven and Serendipity are painted on or carved into wooden signs casually mounted above doors or hung on picket fences, gates and trees.

Along with this distinctive visual came an apparent presence of mind which went back even further. When efforts to maintain a unique appeal were coupled with an unwillingness to see their little village become "citified," the founding fathers rejected home mail delivery in favor of establishing a central post office. As such, house names (considered bad luck to change) along with local coordinates and landmarks act as addresses for visitors or special deliveries. These efforts at preserving an unspoiled simplicity continue to this day with additional bans on chain restaurants, residential sidewalks, parking meters and traffic lights.

Just east of town the scenery changed to a deeply forested inland run through the Point Lobos State Natural Reserve – its name derived from the offshore rocks at Punta de los Lobos Marinos ("Point of the Sea Wolves") – where "the sound of the sea lion carries inland." Although an area rich in headlands, coves and rolling meadows, my only experience was with the road as it led me directly to those mountainside runs seen earlier from Stillwater Cove. When a bright yellow "winding arrow" sign promised several twists and turns for the "Next 74 Miles," I was lit up with anticipation – though short lived.

As scenic drives go along the coast, this still-central leg of the PCH – from the Carmel Highlands to San Simeon – offered more than most. Open spaces and wooded paths suddenly became steep along winding terrain that overlooked the Pacific. No shoreline saunter; it was an obvious contrast to the more manicured roads in Monterey and Carmel. A series of concrete arched bridges along the way (all six built in the early 1930s) only intensified this experience; undoubtedly contributing to its mythic reputation and characterization as "the longest and most scenic stretch of undeveloped coastline in the contiguous United States." Not unlike the Lost Coast back in Humboldt County, there was a stirring sense of isolation on this remarkable pass (which took eighteen years to build). A brief journal entry about all the amazing views – with the intended irony of understatement – seems to sum it up well:

> "Driving along the very edge of the country... 'nothing' but a sheer and towering mass of land blocking everything to my left, a narrow winding road ahead that seems to go on forever and some water to the right. I was really hoping there'd be something more to see out here."

That winding ribbon of road was visible several miles beyond the headlands and offshore rocks and I was once again taken with the notion of visiting my view – especially when the Bixby Creek Bridge (1932) appeared around a blind curve; its profile standing out vividly in the late-afternoon sun. This single-span, concrete, arched bridge is one of the tallest of its kind in the world and one of the most photographed in California due to its "graceful architecture and magnificent setting." From its spectacular side view on approach to the actual 714-foot crossing, it did

125

not disappoint – fittingly closing out the chain of bridges and opening the road to some even-more-engaging terrain.

Crossing the Bixby Creek Bridge toward Big Sur

The mountains here seem to rise abruptly from the water as extremely elevated runs – literally cut into the face of enormous seaside cliffs – snake their way south. As the pull of gravity once again did its part to test my brakes and raise the bar, the twists and turns continued all the way down to a near-sea-level straightaway. There was adventure in the unknown and it was more of what I had come for; every aspect of it a reward. But when a series of bright orange construction signs with their typically unwelcome messages started popping up on the way to my next planned stop – Big Sur – I began to sense that I may get shortchanged on those promised miles. Or worse… have to endure some backtracking.

Setting aside those thoughts for the moment, I allowed the sprawling backdrop to continue lulling me into a state of bliss for several extended and enviable miles. And when a gleaming midnight blue 1965 Mustang approached from the northbound lane, I felt a twinge of envy myself as some thought had been given to renting one for this trek. Although not a "car guy" in any true sense, there was always something about the smooth lines and classic look of those old '65s that appealed to me (or maybe it's just because I'm an old '65). And in that moment – on that equally classic road – the feeling was more palpable than ever. But it was also just as fleeting as the changing scenery and road continued to demand my attention.

Expansive ocean views and outlooks soon gave way to the shade of tall oaks, pines and cypress as they lined the narrow path and tempted me onward. This beautiful valley run in the Santa Lucias was marred only by the increasing number of those signs... "Road Work Ahead," "Rough Road" and ultimately (disappointingly) "Road Closed at Big Sur." A quick check showed that closure to be about twenty miles further along, so I decided to press on. Although fully aware that I'd have to backtrack, my reasoning was twofold: being surrounded by nature was easy to take and the return – which held the possibility of revealing something new – would be no less enjoyable than the drive in. As such, after making it to the large wooden "Pfeiffer Big Sur State Park" sign where I last stopped back in 1986 (this time capturing the moment in the obligatory selfie after a brief stroll among the trees), I turned back the way I came; meandering once more through those woods, across those bridges and along those cliffside runs. And as the shadows grew long across the road, I made my way back to Carmel where I soon found the elegant Carmel Mission Inn – named for the nearby Mission San Carlos Borromeo del Rio Carmelo (1797) – and decided to call it a day.

A quiet dinner at a "gourmet pizzeria" within walking distance of the hotel offered the perfect atmosphere for the usual recount and relaxation – much needed after several stressful minutes of thinking I lost my Jeep keys (eventually found in my room in one of far-too-many pockets on my overnight bag). With the typical din of guests amounting to little more than background noise I sat at the empty bar, pen in hand, attempting to make sense of my notes as the bubbly and smiling Mariana took my drink order and (surprisingly) asked, "Writing anything interesting?"

After a brief pause and a gesture toward the pages in front of me, I could only grin and reply with a considerable twist on a quote about writing that I read long ago by American author Louis L'Amour: "Well, the faucet is on – but I'm not sure how good the water is yet."

NINE

A Place Above

Climb the mountains and get their good tidings

- John Muir

S ome of the more challenging coastal roads in California can be found high above the Pacific in the legendary Topanga Canyon. With its long and storied history as an artistic enclave and with equally celebrated views and terrain, it immediately made my list of must-drive places. In his 2008 autobiography *Heaven and Hell: My Life in The Eagles (1974-2001)* former Eagles guitarist Don Felder made his little piece of the canyon sound so appealing that I bookmarked the page; referring to it nearly ten years later when planning this trip:

"We found a small three-story property set on two acres in a remote part of Topanga Canyon, on a road called Everding Motorway, with spectacular views of the ocean. Set on a steep hill at the end of a dirt road on top of a mountain... we'd fallen in love with the view [but] its only plus was its location. I never tired of the view or watching the fog roll in from the ocean and creep up the valley beneath us and stop, so that we were above the clouds."

With the road closed at Big Sur, my plans to begin the day by running out this coastal stretch of the PCH were shot. I needed to find another thin gray line on the map; one that would help me avoid The 101 and remain lost among the trees. As I traced my finger south along a route through the Santa Lucias and all the way down to the small town of Greenfield, I imagined an agreeable mix of shaded twists and turns accented by a few straightaways – what appeared to be nearly seventy miles of backroad driving.

Perfect.

And although it had the unappealing designation of "G16" on paper, signs soon made it clear that I was rolling along the far more attractive-sounding Carmel Valley Road. This long, meandering, local two-lane lived up to and beyond my expectations offering a host of wonders from oak-shaded stretches of narrow pavement to wide-open expanses where cattle grazed along the rise and fall of gently sloping hills. By contrast, sporadic and steep roadside grades held clusters of immense boulders high above the road where signs once again advised of a "Slide Area." This was always fair warning, of course. But I couldn't help thinking that – short of avoiding them altogether – not much could truly be done to lessen a traveler's vulnerability along these narrow and sometimes precarious passes. More simply stated... there was nowhere to go.

When the trees finally cleared, the landscape seemed as vast as the sky. Far-reaching views across pastures looked down into a distant valley where a mountainous backdrop claimed the horizon east beyond Greenfield. While passing through this small community suitably nestled among acres of vineyards I harmonized with the radio; most memorably with Neil Young on "Heart of Gold." As one of the earliest songs to spark my eventual interest in music it was also a favorite that, perhaps somewhat suitably, seemed to be an ode to self-discovery. And even though the lyrics about having been to Hollywood and Redwood spoke offhandedly to this ramble down the coast, Young's metaphorical response to the song's success many years ago seemed to align even more with my reasons for keeping to the back roads:

> "This song put me in the middle of the road. Traveling there soon became a bore so I headed for the ditch. A rougher ride but I saw more interesting people there."

Although I, too, found myself in the middle of the road (The 101) at the far end of those seventy miles, it was a surprisingly pastoral run without any apparent reason to head for the ditch. But where the miles of lush green farmlands turned to a more sunburnt and barren landscape just north of the San Luis Obispo County line so, too, did the highway take on a more desperate look and feel. Too much of that was sure to disappoint – especially knowing that something better certainly awaited me off the beaten path. Stopping in the very next town (San Miguel), I fueled up while once again scanning my map in the hope that a more tempting route back to the coast would be *revealed* to me. This time it came by way of a thicker gray line (a "through road") about fifteen miles south that seemed to cross the southernmost end of the Santa Lucias and run all the way out to the PCH.

Gesturing to an older gentleman at the next pump whom I assumed to be a local by his California plates and who just stepped back into his nearly equally older pickup truck, I casually asked if he thought Highway 46 would be my best bet to the coast.

131

"Not if you wanna get there quicker," he said with the pleasant, almost-stereotypical delivery of an experienced old-timer. "Just stay on 101 for about thirty miles and pick up 41 in Atascadero – takes you right to the bay."

Of course, quicker was never part of the plan and "the bay" was the small waterfront city of Morro Bay. Although previously on my radar after a planned pass through Big Sur, it marked the end of the coastal PCH for a while and would have been pointless to race there only to turn inland again.

"Thanks," I said with a wave as he simply nodded and drove off.

Though only a brief encounter, I found his manner intriguing. My journal entry about the exchange (which included a note about that melodic name Atascadero – "to be stuck or hindered" – perhaps best I avoided it) ended with: "… a deadpan delivery that evoked a sort of down-home 'Ya can't get there from here' charisma. Sincere, obliging, noble, amusing, salt of the earth – genuine."

Highway 46 in Paso Robles ("the pass of the oaks") is known locally as Green Valley Road – and for good reason. As with Wine Road back in the Anderson Valley it rolls through miles of fertile vineyards and wineries – all part of the booming Paso Robles Wine Country. Its realization is said to be owed in part to the unique blends created by viticulturists who tend to flout traditional rules of winemaking. Perhaps a nod to the creativity involved in the process of that craft. One which many consider an art form no different than that of, say, a chef or a brewmaster. Which brings to mind many quotes about discovery, making your own path and the like. But Spanish artist Pablo Picasso may have said it best (offering some sound advice at the outset): "Learn the rules like a pro, so you can break them like an artist."

The array of neatly lined grapevines blanketing the hills of Paso Robles is a show of viticultural artistry – both practical and pleasing. Where the vineyards end, a stand of Douglas firs, coast redwoods and ponderosa pines gradually ushers the road back into the mountains. Climbing to more than

1800 feet, it passes over the range in a laid-back ramble of soft curves and occasional outlooks offering long views of the descent ahead. Once again, the decision to avoid those concrete slashes of highway paying off nicely.

Eventually arriving at the PCH along a coastal buffer of golden hills that kept the Pacific at bay and from view, I was intrigued by a small sign directing me two miles south toward "Harmony" and immediately set my sights accordingly. Upon arrival, however, I discovered that there was almost no "there" there and it reminded me of a D.H. Lawrence quote about scenic travel that has long resonated with me: "That's the place to get to – nowhere."

As the sign just outside of town would suggest ("Harmony - Pop 18"), it was little more than a single road less than a quarter-mile long with no evidence of that supposed population visible at the time. Despite a small winery up the hill serving as an impressive backdrop in this otherwise quiet and isolated setting, Old Creamery Road had only a couple of very small homes at one end and a business or two at the other (yes, one a creamery). It made Leggett back in Mendocino County seem like a metropolis with its population of 120.

When the coastal buffer receded several miles downcoast the ocean view was accompanied by noticeably cooler air all the way to the seaside town of Cayucos ("dugout kayak"). Morro Rock in the distance – a remarkable sight at nearly 600 feet tall – announced its namesake city long before any manmade sign had the chance. Perched at the mouth of its harbor and home to nesting Peregrine falcons (the fastest animal on Earth with a "rapid stoop" dive for prey that can top 200 miles per hour), this State Historic Landmark (1968) sits northernmost in a chain of nine volcanic peaks from San Luis Obispo to Morro Bay known as the Nine Sisters. A sacred site to the Salinan and Chumash Tribes who once populated parts of San Luis Obispo and other central and southern California regions, it is said to be the focus of many Salinan legends. One of which – The Legend of the Serpent – tells dramatically of the time when a falcon and a raven destroyed "the terrible two-headed serpent monster Taliyekatapelta" as he wrapped his body around the base of the rock.

With no two-headed serpents visible on this day, I continued inland past a few more 'Sisters, through the county seat of San Luis Obispo and back out to the coast at "Classic California Pismo Beach" – so announced a large and "beachy" gateway monument at the edge of town. Finding a little seafood place (The Flagship) along the water allowed me to reflect on my day and consider the route ahead all with a peaceful view of the ocean just beyond the top of my menu.

Each of these stops so far had been an opportunity to decompress, add color and clarity to my notes and otherwise smell the proverbial roses. And when these breaks were along the water they seemed to become Zen-like moments of meditation. I stayed a little longer, thought a little deeper and felt a little more relaxed when I finally decided to get back on the road – which was typically "whenever." I discovered early on that an open-ended journey lends itself well to the traveler who wishes to remain truly present throughout. Without time constraints or any true agenda to adhere to (or inhibit), letting the here-and-now wash over me became very easy rather quickly. Bryson details the inherent appeal of this travel-without-restrictions in *A Walk in the Woods*:

> "Life takes on a neat simplicity, too. Time ceases to have any meaning. When it is dark, you go to bed, and when it is light again, you get up, and everything in between is just in between. It's quite wonderful, really. You have no engagements, commitments, obligations, or duties; no special ambitions and only the smallest, least complicated of wants; you exist in a tranquil tedium, serenely beyond the reach of exasperation, 'far removed from the seats of strife,' as the early explorer and botanist William Bartram put it. All that is required of you is a willingness to trudge. There is no point in hurrying because you are not actually going anywhere."

As the sound of Jimmy Buffett's "One Particular Harbor" played overhead, I stared out at the restaurant's little staged shipwreck in the sand and wondered if playing his music (and some of the other "Yacht Rock" songs I heard while there) was a deliberate attempt by management to sell the seafaring atmosphere to customers. Of course, as a fan of both Buffett and the genre I had no objection. Nevertheless, all the nautical indulgence just seemed so... flawless. And yet, as the kindly Marissa walked away after having taken my order, my notes lay untouched on the table for a time as I continued staring out at the water and singing along to myself – clearly taken in by the very vibe I was questioning... *"But there's this one particular harbor, so far but yet so near, where I see the days as they fade away and finally disappear..."*

A southeast run along the valley floor crossed the Santa Barbara County line on the outskirts of Santa Maria – its most populous city. A mix of deep green vineyards, small settlements and golden rolling hills made the drive from Pismo Beach to the Santa Ynez Valley easy on the eyes – not to mention the ears. Expressive town names like the Chumash Arroyo Grande ("wide riverbed") and Nipomo ("foot of the hills"), the Spanish-Mexican Los Alamos ("the cottonwoods") and Los Olivos ("the olive trees") and even the Danish Solvang ("sunny field") all pointed to the richness of the landscape and the culturally diverse history along this part of the coast.

The Chumash Highway headed directly toward the Santa Ynez Mountains in the Transverse Ranges and into the southwest corner of the Los Padres National Forest – a "Land of Many Uses," according to its sign. This chain of mountains is so-named for its east-west orientation running more than 300 miles from southwestern Santa Barbara County eastward into the Mojave and Colorado Deserts. When intermittent views of Lake Cachuma to my left were suddenly contradicted by an alarming expanse of scorched earth to my right, I had confirmation of the faint and ironically pleasing scent noticed only moments earlier – like a snuffed-out bonfire in summer. Even though I had read about many coastal wildfires and the ruin left in their wake, actually passing through an area affected by one is far more jarring. The forest floor – still gray with ash – showed no sign of its usually dense layer of brushwood and the trunks of thinned-out oaks were blackened to their canopies; many fallen in defeat. Appearing to have been a relatively fresh burn, I made a note to look into it.

The charred aftermath along the Chumash Highway

Named after its origin in a nearby campsite, the Whittier Fire started only one month prior to my pass through and had yet to be completely contained. Although wildfires often have devastating and comprehensive effects (this one burned more than 18,370 acres and destroyed more than forty-five homes and buildings), they also have ecological benefits considered necessary to the health of forests. Just as the clearing of underbrush and decaying plants helps return nutrients to the soil so, too, does the reduced canopy coverage allow sunlight to reach the ground encouraging new growth. But all of this is a relatively slow process as the immediate effects on wildlife and landscape are typically widespread taking several years to reverse.

Beyond the fire's footprint a more pristine display of deep-green oaks began to dot the hillside as an array of vibrant Spanish broom plants lined the road; their bright yellow blooms unusually full in late summer as if in defiance of the recent fire. Planted along Southern California roadsides in the 1920s, they now dominate the landscape and fill the air with a strong, sweet fragrance – perhaps more noticeable to me as I had just come through those charred remains. As the path slowly became more shrouded in trees I could feel the effects of its ascent into the Santa Ynez Range. Crossing the Cold Spring Canyon Bridge at 1600 feet, I was rewarded with panoramic views southwest over treetops and northeast across distant peaks. Opening to the public in 1963, this 1200-foot span over a tree-filled ravine – once a stagecoach stop – was considered a feat of engineering, design and beauty and is still the highest arch bridge in California at 400 feet above the canyon floor.

Named for Marcos Amestoy, a monk who ran Mission Santa Barbara (known as "Queen of the Missions") in the early 1800s, San Marcos Pass crossed the summit largely unannounced at approximately 2230 feet. Although easily evident by the feel of the road and its relief on the Jeep's engine, the only visual indication of having reached this point was a small sign showing a truck on a steep decline and beneath it the warning: "Next 8 Miles." Fortunately much of that trek was more of what I'd just experienced – only in reverse. A beautifully forested and winding downhill run that tested the brakes with sluggish speed limits and occasionally expansive views across the divide or out to the Pacific. As the trees naturally thinned in the foothills beyond those more severe descents, the highway slowly returned to sea level just east of the upscale community of Hope Ranch. A reconnection with the PCH in the county seat of Santa Barbara eventually brought me to a more relaxing coastal drive; the ocean glistening beside me and Santa Cruz Island – the largest of the eight Channel Islands – visible in the hazy distance. The combination of cloudless skies and an easy run along the water made for an agreeable complement to the mountain pass. Just as the musical element of tension-and-release eventually dissolves the buildup into a more relaxed rhythm, it was a timely change of pace and scenery once again welcome.

It was this continually varying landscape that added an appealing element of chance to all these roads less traveled. Whether a forested inland run with random twists and turns or a straightaway through open farms and fields, a slow meander along a narrow valley floor or an extended and swerving shoreline drive – the uncertainty of what was ahead seemed the perfect way to experience this wide-ranging coast. Each time I rounded a bend, crossed a bridge or emerged from another ramble through the trees my immediate thought was that persistent and eager *"What next?"*

Just south of the Ventura County line begins the nearly eighty-mile long Ventura Freeway – at times simultaneously the Pacific Coast Highway, U.S. Route 101 and the Historic El Camino Real; as marked by several more roadside mission bells. It's also part of California's 240-mile stretch of the Purple Heart Trail extending from Monterey County to Ventura County. This nationwide program established in 1992 honors United States military personnel who have been awarded the Purple Heart for their service and sacrifice to our country (just as the Blue Star Memorial Highways have paid tribute to members of the armed forces since 1945). Originating at a monument in Mount Vernon, Virginia (George Washington's burial site) the unconnected trail currently has representation in forty-five states as well as the United States island territory of Guam.

Despite all these formal designations, as I made my way south along the freeway toward Ventura – officially the City of San Buenaventura – I felt as if I was driving along the fictionalized "Ventura Highway" lyrically depicted in America's 1972 hit of the same name (the sunshine, longer days and stronger nights noted in the chorus somewhat suggestive of a recent study which ranked the county as "most scenic" in the country). Signs for Ventura Harbor and Ventura Pier amid a growing number of swaying fan palms and sandy beaches aroused long-held visions not unlike those imagined in the song. Inspired by a childhood memory of a coastal California drive and written from the perspective of one day leaving the cold Omaha winters behind, singer Lee Martin "Dewey" Bunnell spoke to a sort of escapism through his lyrics as explained in the liner notes of America's 2000 album *Highway: 30 Years of America*:

> "There were cold winters and I had images of going to California. So I think in the song I'm talking to myself… I remember vividly having this mental picture of the stretch of the coastline traveling with my family when I was younger. Ventura Highway itself, there is no such beast, what I was really trying to depict was the Pacific Coast Highway, Highway 1, which goes up to the town of Ventura."

After quietly making my way through inland Ventura (home to Mission San Buenaventura – "The Mission by the Sea") and cutting across open farmland on the outskirts of Oxnard, I returned to the coast at Point Mugu State Park along the northern tip of the Santa Monica Mountains. As the song ran through my mind the ocean once again offered up its charms and for the next forty wonderful miles an offshore breeze circulated throughout the cabin. The radio would eventually be turned on to end the musical refrain in my head. But in the meantime I allowed the lyrical imagery to become part of my reality as I rolled down the PCH en route to Topanga Canyon… *"Ventura Highway in the sunshine, where the days are longer, the nights are stronger than moonshine…"*

I crossed the Los Angeles County line several miles north of Zuma Beach where a sign depicting the coastline asserted rather confidently: "Malibu - 21 Miles of Scenic Beauty." I was always hopeful that the reality would live up to the claim on signs like this. And even though the drive into town wasn't quite as picturesque as expected (or as it would be further downcoast), the colonized foothills, ocean views and long stretches of beach – some awash in a pageantry of colorful umbrellas – were hardly eyesores. The name Malibu is derived from the Chumash "Humaliwo" ("where the surf sounds loudly" – the "Hu" silent). And with its status as a mecca of surf culture since the late '60s, it has certainly lived up to the name. At the southern end of Zuma Beach sits California Historical Landmark No. 965 – Point Dume; a large, 200-foot-tall cape that juts out into the ocean and marks the western end of Santa Monica Bay. Although named in 1793 for Father Francisco Dumetz of Mission San Buenaventura (1782), various maps from the early 1800s show his surname alternately misspelled as "Dume" and "Zuma." Never corrected, the names endured.

Having read that Point Dume was actually a volcanic cone, I was expecting a large and barren rock formation sitting at the water's edge. Upon arrival at its base, however, I was met with more of a coastal meadow; a chaparral-covered expanse running from the beach to the street and designated the "Point Dume Natural Preserve." The customary information sign at the trailhead noted that "everything from butterflies to coyotes" inhabited this "small tract of land" and that they were highly adaptable to its sometimes-harsh living conditions. Given their noted resilience, it was surprising to also read that this same wildlife was extremely vulnerable to simple domesticated dogs as the scent they leave behind "can disrupt breeding or foraging behavior for weeks." This clearly explained and validated another nearby sign – its message at the center of many ongoing debates regarding public parks and spaces: "No Dogs Allowed."

Where the wave-cut cliffs soften just east of Point Dume, the PCH gradually falls to a mostly sea-level run following the contour of the coast. The countless homes that line this stretch of shoreline from just west of Malibu Lagoon State Beach are densely packed, relatively small and yet some of the most expensive real estate in Los Angeles. The most notable among these homes are found in Malibu Colony. This once privately owned, mile-long strip of land (now a modestly gated but upscale community) was the first local beachfront property to be developed when it was opened to the public back in 1929. Celebrated for its setting and views, it quickly attracted a Who's Who of Hollywood's elite and soon after was informally christened "Malibu Movie Colony." But there was little enjoyment in the drive just east of Malibu Pier (1905) where an uninviting and confining stretch of residential and commercial congestion completely belied any hint of the scenery I had passed through only moments before. This unbroken line of homes and businesses encroached on the road for several miles before welcome views of open land and sea finally returned at Highway 27 – more appealingly known as Topanga Canyon Boulevard. My gateway (or getaway) to the Santa Monica Mountains.

Just off the PCH at the mouth of the canyon lies a narrow, one-mile stretch of sand called Topanga Beach. With its sweeping view of Santa Monica Bay it seemed another perfect spot to pull over and appreciate this journey as reward. To pause for a bit and, again, be in the moment. Once my toes were buried in the warm sand I felt immersed in the coast. Just as I had when walking among the giants in Humboldt Redwood State Park or relaxing amid the grapevines of the Anderson Valley. These were more than just moments of repose; more than just being in the forest, at the vineyard or on the beach. They were opportunities to reflect; to capture the finer points of this experience and even to document them in real time. Another passage from Emerson's *Nature* spoke well to this deeper connection to our natural surroundings:

> "When we speak of nature in this manner, we have a distinct but most poetical sense in the mind. We mean the integrity of impression made by manifold natural objects. It is this which distinguishes the stick of timber of the wood-cutter, from the tree of the poet."

From the outlet of Topanga Creek at the western end to the rocky foreland that bounds it in the east, Topanga Beach proved a fine respite from the road. With the call of seagulls and lapping waves once again serving as background music, I caught a faint profile of the Palos Verdes Peninsula at the far end of the bay while scanning the horizon for a glimpse of Santa Catalina Island some twenty miles offshore. Although third largest of the eight Channel Islands, Catalina is the only one with a sizable and permanent settlement; the resort town of Avalon – the southernmost city "in" Los Angeles County.

Turning from the beach I began my scramble up Topanga Canyon Boulevard into this land once sacred to the indigenous Tongva tribe (as was Catalina) – Topanga Canyon. In addition to being named in reference to their village site being above the high water of the creek, I discovered that Topanga ("a place above") was an old Shoshonean word that also – and rather aptly – alluded to the sky or heaven.

As with its countercultural cousin Laurel Canyon to the east, this one-time bohemian haven on the outskirts of Los Angeles is as well known for its rustic landscape as for its musical heritage. Songs by Neil Young, The Doors and Eagles guitarist Don Felder, among others, were inspired by experiences in these hills and my trek into their historic folds was encouraged, in part, by Felder's captivating description of his first home being "set on a steep hill at the end of a dirt road on top of a mountain." This sounded so isolated and nearly unreachable that even on the page it was music to my ears. As discovered while passing through the extremely remote Lost Coast back in Humboldt and Mendocino Counties, disappearing into such a beautifully complex landscape could be intriguing. And the notion of getting there – as always – even more so.

At once surrounded by oak trees and outcrops, this winding two-lane pass held a promise of reward that improved commensurately with each gain in elevation. Even though the beauty of the setting was obvious, little roadside signs with a logo of the California poppy set against snow-capped peaks appeared every so often – an indication that this was officially a

"State Scenic Highway." Various vista-point views reached far and wide across the canyon where a brilliant blue sky faded to white along the horizon. Clearly visible dirt trails hugged the steep and harsh terrain of sister mountains, cutting across vertical bare protrusions and winding their way up to those distant summits. More immediately the road became an endless array of bends – tight, narrow and precarious – where hairpin turns, steep embankments and inclines were often negotiated simultaneously. Along the more meandering and constricted upper reaches, where center lines were no longer painted on the road and guardrails were intermittent, signs reminded of "Two Way Traffic" while others recommended a fifteen-mile-per-hour speed limit – the slowest yet in my travels.

Perhaps most puzzling was that this was actually a residential neighborhood, though hardly your typical subdivision. These roads I was scrabbling on were a daily commute to those who call this rugged terrain home. And yet I shared them with very few cars at the lower elevations and none along higher, more challenging passes. Of course, having the road to myself was always a luxury, especially on a scenic drive. But it seemed almost a necessity along this combination of tapering twists and turns where keeping eyes on the road and hands on the wheel were more than just offhand poetic sentiments by The Doors as it was this very pass that Jim Morrison was referring to when he wrote the lyrics for "Roadhouse Blues" in 1969.

Sitting roadside at the base of Felder's former property, the uniquely shaped home still standing and occupied (by Marvin Gaye at one time), I thought about the relative inaccessibility of this area and how it must have seemed even more remote when he lived here in the mid '70s just as the Eagles began soaring. Although the view was as he described, after venturing a few hundred yards further up a desolate dirt road and stopping at an even more-elevated, south-facing bluff I was able to get a better sense of what that may have been like. Sweeping views of adjacent peaks were blanketed by a deep green forest that began seemingly at my feet – the ocean visible just beyond. I once read that it can be unsettling

143

to find yourself in a beautiful place when you can't linger... and when traveling through the mountains one thing you can be sure of is that there will always be more mountains. Fortunately, as a light but steady breeze attempted to cool the effects of the late-afternoon sun, I had plenty of time to stand in silent wonder at the top of all of this perfection and just take it all in knowing one day these experiences would be distant memories. Recalling that moment and those views for this story brought to mind a brief passage from Muir's 1911 work *My First Summer in the Sierra*:

> "The more rugged and inaccessible the general character
> of the topography of any particular region, the more surely
> will the trails... be found converging into the best passes."

One of those passes on this drive was Tuna Canyon Road – a mostly one-way downhill heading out of the canyon and back to the PCH just west of Topanga Canyon Boulevard. While this gravity-fueled run twisted and turned its way south through some steep and treacherous landscape, my hands remained firmly "upon the wheel" as I hoped to gain confidence through trial – not error. Although occasional signs for "Winding Road" were always welcome, other familiar warnings about "Rock Slide Area" and "One Way" seemed generally unhelpful as any opportunities to dodge rocks or errant traffic along this narrow track appeared limited at best. In the clearing around each bend the vanishing points of distant hills offered quick visual hints of the continued descent. But where the trees began to close in at lower elevations those views were lost and the road simultaneously tapered to little more than a glorified bike path through the increasingly dense foliage. Even though it was an amazingly enjoyable drive all throughout the Santa Monicas, this relatively straight and level finish was a welcome respite – almost a reward. And as the coast drew near on that final mile I was able to relax my grip on the wheel, ease up on the brakes and unwind effortlessly through the shadows of sycamores, alders and willows.

After some random wandering through the lush and affluent hills of Pacific Palisades and along Santa Monica's beachfront Ocean Avenue (and following a few failed attempts in my usual late-day search for a place to spend the night), I reluctantly allowed the road to lead me back to Malibu where I found a room at the top of The Malibu Hotel. Staying right on the busy PCH offered the somewhat unusual pairing of an ocean view with the sound of traffic at night. The latter evoking childhood memories of summer visits with my maternal grandparents in their fourth-floor, walk-up apartment on the Upper West Side of Manhattan. Those open windows on 204th Street allowed for occasional firetruck sirens, car horns and other random sounds to play through the rooms in a medley of echoes from the New York streets below – all intriguing to a child's ears. Each of those visits to the "big city" provided a dramatic and audibly stimulating change of pace from the more natural and quiet surroundings of our suburban South Jersey home some two hours away. But my brother, three sisters and I learned quickly how to sleep through all of it.

In his 2015 autobiography *Over the Top and Back*, Welsh singer Sir Tom Jones wrote similarly of an experience he had in 1965 during his first trip to New York for an appearance on the Ed Sullivan Show:

> "It's the song that has carried me to New York, where I will lie in bed with the windows thrown open so that I can hear the distinctive honking of the taxis in the streets way below, a soundtrack familiar to me from the movies and now made real."

I walked to a local bistro for a late and casual dinner (the requisite pictures of celebrity customers on the walls) before heading back to the room to put in some considerable homework time, check in with Kell and, ultimately, call it a day. Stepping out onto the balcony I caught that final tawny glow of sunset as it made a silhouette of the foothills to the west and faded over the Pacific. Watching and listening as the headlights and taillights sped up and down the highway, I was reminded of how agreeable that familiar sound was to me. And as darkness fell more completely over the coast I stepped back inside to settle in with my Kindle – the balcony door left open to allow the "soundtrack" of the street below to drift in… as I drifted off.

The sights (and sounds) of the PCH at night

TEN

Beneath the Hills

Be always searching for new sensations

~ Oscar Wilde

Traffic was already heavy on the PCH as I looked down from my balcony dreading that I would soon be part of it. Although the memory of seeing those cliffside palms and white-sand beaches on the way to Santa Monica was appealing on this warm sunny morning, the thought of voluntarily joining rush-hour traffic was far less so. After all, one of the luxuries of this open-ended trek was having no time constraints. And taking the road *more* traveled was never part of the plan. All the same, committed to making the most of the daylight hours I concededly chalked it up as a necessary evil and forged ahead into this somewhat lesser version of that notorious "L.A. traffic."

As demanding as it was – certainly more so than most of what I'd experienced along this coast so far – it was soon matched in adrenaline by a favorite classic from The Hollies ("Long Cool Woman in a Black Dress") that had me singing along, dashboard drumming and (almost) oblivious to the surrounding crush of commuters... *"Saturday night I was downtown, working for the FBI, sittin' in a nest of bad men, whiskey bottles piling high..."*

If coastal runs, forested back roads and winding mountain passes reflected my ideal for scenic driving, then music proved the perfect complement as both companion and inspiration. And with an ongoing interest in seeing or being where certain events happened or were inspired, I set my sights accordingly. Loosely mapping out my course in the months prior, I added some secondary places as possible stops either along the way or within a reasonable distance of the coast (however undefined that may have been) to casually explore some landscapes of a different sort.

One of those stops was the otherwise unremarkable intersection of Lincoln and Olympic Boulevards less than a mile east of Santa Monica Beach. With no obvious indication of any cultural or historical significance apart from two small signs on opposite traffic lights ("End" and "Begin"), I realized that this – the official westernmost end of the classic and legendary Route 66 – was not as popular as its more "spiritual" end on the famed Santa Monica Pier (1909). It was there where a more impressive and pronounced sign stood tall against the Pacific hinting at the old tale of how this spirited and historic road only ended when the sea stood in its way ("Santa Monica - 66 - End of the Trail"). Surrounded by tourists in "selfie mode," it was clearly more of a draw than some busy street corner. Regardless, I chose to believe the absence of any fanfare at that inland crossroads was due to its true appeal actually belonging to all the miles that unfurled to the east – those celebrated in movies, music and literature.

Steeped in nostalgia and symbolic of restlessness since its opening in 1926, the nearly 2500-mile Route 66 – from the Pacific Ocean to the shores of Monroe Harbor in Lake Michigan – has been the setting of countless tales of travel and adventure; often a mingling of fact and fiction. As "the mother road, the road of flight" in Steinbeck's *The Grapes of Wrath* it was an escape to the hopes and dreams of a better life during the Dust Bowl years of the 1930s. In Jack Kerouac's semi-autobiographical *On the Road* it was emblematic of freedom in 1940's and 1950's America. And in 1968 the cult classic *Easy Rider* was filmed along some of those unfurled miles as a pair of "biker-hippie" protagonists headed east toward New Orleans in search of spiritual truth during the Vietnam-era '60s.

For more than thirty years this "Main Street of America" was considered *"the highway that's the best,"* as Bobby Troup sings in his 1946 hit song "(Get Your Kicks) On Route 66." But when the Interstate Highway Act was signed by President Eisenhower in 1956, a slow and steady grind toward its formal decommission began. Although the actual road and many of its celebrated attractions are still present along those original miles, with most of the bypasses complete by 1985 it was effectively and officially retired. Soon after this demotion it began disappearing from maps and other travel guides – the ghostly beauty of those old stretches more permanently etched in the past and only occasionally noted along the roadside (or boldly painted right on the asphalt) as "Historic Route 66."

But its enduring romance and distinctive role among travelers appealed to my interest in being in that place, however marginally. And so it was that I spent some time walking its westernmost end in an effort to see it, feel it and simply be there – both officially and spiritually.

Sunset Boulevard is another storied run snaking for twenty-two miles from the coast at Pacific Palisades east through Beverly Hills and into downtown Los Angeles. A far cry from its days as an old cattle trail in the early 1800s, much of it is now a seemingly endless tunnel of foliage. Lavish homes in nearly every architectural style sit quietly on pristine lawns behind gated driveways and empty sidewalks – all beneath the infamous

Mulholland Drive in the shadow of both Topanga and Laurel Canyons. The evenly spaced ficus trees, border hedges and tall fan palms that line the way are scenic in their own right. And despite this being an otherwise well-traveled path – especially a small section formerly named Beverly Boulevard – my drive was easy and unrushed. What it lacked in solitude it more than made up for in splendor as the filtered sunlight created a peaceful effect on the landscape (and perhaps on the drivers as well).

As the distinctive blush façade of the Beverly Hills Hotel (1912) appeared through the trees, the opening lines of Sheryl Crow's 1994 hit "All I Wanna Do" seemed to underscore the moment with a timely pronouncement... *"This ain't no disco, it ain't no country club either, this is L.A..."* Though the merging of good songs on road trips always offers an opportunity to become further engrossed in the experience, there was no getting lost in this one as the sight of the "Pink Palace" immediately transported me to an image and song dating back more than forty years.

The cover of the Eagles 1976 album *Hotel California* was a dark, slightly obscured shot of the Beverly Hills Hotel set against the bright burn of twilight. And though my view on approach was from a slightly different angle, as is said in music circles "it was close enough for rock'n'roll" – like the album cover come to life. Bright red curbs and impeccable greenery bordered the long, curved driveway as the three olive-green domes of the hotel's Mediterranean Revival architecture slowly came into view. Perched high above the surrounding palms their white spires now fly the flags of the United States, California and Mexico. Although the cover art was the only connection between band and building, the multi-platinum success of both the album (recorded at the same time as *Rumours*) and its title track (named Record of the Year in 1977) soon made the hotel synonymous with the song and therefore an easy addition to my travel plans. After poking around the "lovely" grounds for a while and taking it all in, I headed toward the less manicured, more commercial and far grittier part of the boulevard known as the Sunset Strip where I would continue for a while on foot; ambling along its musical path.

Hotel California… such a lovely place

The slow transformation from Beverly Hills to West Hollywood went almost unnoticed until I was actually there amid the billboards, buildings and bars – everything that belies those earlier, more natural surroundings along Sunset. When the well-maintained foliage along the median disappeared, it was a clear and sudden indication that I was on The Strip – that nearly two-mile section of the boulevard that has been cemented in the history of rock'n'roll since the mid-1960s (with former and varied incarnations dating back to the '20s). A defining moment in that history came by way of protest in late 1966 when curfews and efforts to close local nightclubs encouraged what was to be a peaceful demonstration outside the popular hangout Pandora's Box (1962). Sparking days of unrest the ultimately unruly incident came to be known as The Sunset Strip Riots. In response to all the observed confusion and turmoil, Buffalo Springfield's Stephen Stills wrote "For What It's Worth (Stop, Hey What's That Sound)." Even if the lyrics were open to interpretation, the overall message seemed to sum up the mood of the country at the time – perhaps having a lasting impact or a renewed claim on present day... *"There's somethin' happening here, what it is ain't exactly clear…"*

Although one of Sunset's pioneering rock clubs – Gazzarri's (1967) – was long gone (as with the Starwood on Santa Monica Boulevard), others that gave rise to some of the biggest bands of the previous four decades were still alive and well (like the Troubadour also on Santa Monica). But most of them appeared to blend in to the more conventional surroundings remaining mostly unchanged over time – the legendary Rainbow Bar & Grill (1972), the Roxy Theater (1973) and to a lesser extent the Whisky a Go Go (1964). The Viper Room (1993) – with its long history as The Last Call, The Cotton Club and The Melody Room, among others – was the exception with its edgier and more sinister all-black façade. This perhaps a holdover image from its most recent previous incarnation as Filthy McNasty's – a 1970's rock club frequented in the early days by everyone from Elvis Presley to Little Richard; from Mick Jagger to John Wayne – all of whom were said to have appreciated the owner's ban on cameras. Though all these clubs certainly characterized the true spirit of The Strip, the essence of its musical culture was also visible in other ways and I rounded out this more urban scenic tour by taking note of a few.

The familiar red and yellow presence of Tower Records (1969) stood out as I approached the corner of Sunset Boulevard & Horn Avenue. Although now closed in a sign of the times, it was such a powerful image for both the vibe of the boulevard and the musicians it attracted that the city maintained its large and iconic signage for more than a decade after its closing. When Don Henley first sang about the "Sunset Grill" in 1985 it evoked in me images of a simple little burger stand on a sidewalk somewhere in sunny California. More than thirty years later I discovered it was actually a cozy little eatery flanked by an array of music stores, coffee bars and book shops. Even Sunset Sound recording (1962) appeared modest and small both in contrast to what I imagined and to its remarkable list of clients – from Led Zeppelin, The Rolling Stones and Van Halen to Bob Dylan, Paul McCartney, Elton John, the Beach Boys and Barbra Streisand among many others.

It seemed no matter where I wandered beneath the Hollywood Hills, there was always some tangible evidence of pop-cultural history enticing me to stop; to look around and be *there* – many of them worth that enticement. Each closer look offering a different perspective, some small discovery or even a new experience or sensation. The bright white turrets and towers of the famed Chateau Marmont Hotel (1929) looming high just off Sunset. The circular, album-like floors of the venerable Capitol Records Building (1956) – a standout on Vine. Even distant views of the classic Hollywood sign (1923) overlooking the City of Angels from Mount Lee. All of these and more provided a backdrop for countless stories that became the stuff of legend; some celebrated, others tragic. And those stories all began somewhere – one aspect of any undertaking that always intrigued me. The start of all things great and small has a tendency to inspire and rejuvenate; encouraging effort over apathy, conquest over adversity and interest over indifference.

The world's first circular office building

It was that same fascination and curiosity which led me on a slight detour from West Hollywood to Pasadena ("crown of the valley") for a few moments of reflection in front of the childhood home of the musically renowned Van Halen brothers – drummer Alex and guitarist Eddie (who passed away during this writing). My visit was simply to see it; to get a sense of place for their beginnings after they emigrated from Amsterdam and before they landed on the world stage behind the success of their namesake band Van Halen (which quickly began influencing countless young hopefuls; this drummer among them). On the small tract of land behind the pale yellow rancher sits a modest backyard-shed-turned-rehearsal-space. It was there where the two budding musicians would eventually hone their crafts and where the classically trained pianist would soon become a guitar prodigy who would redefine how the instrument was played – making that little shed a mostly unrecognized yet noteworthy part of the larger rock'n'roll landscape. My time here, although brief, was another favorable moment of being where something personally meaningful, influential or otherwise significant happened. Sometimes these visits deepen earlier connections. Other times they simply add a cool little flourish to the memories. But every now and then they check both boxes.

Sitting in the shade beneath a canopy of maple trees reminded me of the more natural scenery I was eager to get back to. Turning my attention to that trusty (yet increasingly unwieldy) map in the passenger's seat, I opened it to begin searching for a scenic route out of town. But this time I scanned the coast for an ideal destination first. It was this aspect of my journey that I found most appealing – winging it. Just as there were no true restrictions on my time, neither were there any highlighted roads nor plotted courses on my map. No, this oversized piece of paper with its web of squiggly-lines and numbered signs was used strictly for alternate routes when the road either ended or was closed. Or, as now, when I reached yet another waypoint destination and my only thought (and option) was once again a very motivated *"What next?"*

In *Travels with Charley* Steinbeck expresses some opinions about overzealous mappers – taking them to task while simultaneously extolling the virtues of truly wandering:

> "There are map people whose joy is to lavish more attention on the sheets of colored paper than on the colored land rolling by. Another kind of traveler requires to know in terms of maps exactly where he is pin-pointed every moment, as though there were some kind of safety in black and red lines. It is not so with me. I was born lost and take no pleasure in being found…"

Though I found another stop that looked and sounded worthy, I quickly discovered that any hope of getting there enjoyably would be a bit of a challenge. The course my finger traced this time would have me disposing of several miles along three consecutive and mostly lackluster highways. A necessary evil, a means to an end, this too shall pass – all the usual platitudes apply here. And with those in mind a twist on an old rhyming proverb about the *incurable* also seems fitting… "What can't be *changed* must be endured."

Waving the figurative white flag once again, I resigned myself to another stretch of concrete. The nearby on-ramp to Highway 210 took me east toward San Bernardino – my only hope for getting back to the coast without zigging and zagging through the sluggish clutter of neighborhood streets. Known more commonly to locals as the Foothill Freeway, its one saving grace was that all eighty-five-miles ran parallel to the San Gabriel Mountains to the north; another stretch in the Transverse Ranges. As the sun played off the mountains' countless folds and peaks giving them shadow, color and life, they became a sight for sore eyes making this otherwise featureless setting (surprisingly) more bearable. To that end, even more appealing was a section of the Orange Freeway (Highway 57) that crossed into Orange County during a brief pass through the Santa Ana Mountains. Once more it was that play of light washing over the greens and tans of the coastal sage scrub blanketing the surrounding hills which offered a literal and figurative bright side to this run – and another welcome break from the rest of the highway's visual tedium of… gray.

Residents along this part of the coast have somewhat of a love-hate relationship with one aspect of its weather as it's here in *The Land of Little Rain* – as Mary Hunter Austin titled her 1903 book about Southern California – where those infamous Santa Ana winds sweep down after rolling in from the Great Basin to the east. Although very often clearing the air of impurities and bringing about bright blue skies and stunning sunsets, the darker side of those gusts tends to be a harbinger of ill will – as referenced metaphorically in Steely Dan's equally dark 1980 song, "Babylon Sisters"… *"Here come those Santa Ana winds again…"* This stormy alter ego of sorts is why they're likewise referred to as the diablo ("devil") winds. In addition to literally fanning the flames during California's fire season they're also said to have an equally sinister influence on the behaviors of locals. In his 1938 short story, *Red Wind*, American-British author Raymond Chandler famously described a windy Santa Ana night:

> "There was a desert wind blowing that night. It was one
> of those hot dry Santa Anas that come down through the
> mountain passes and curl your hair and make your nerves
> jump and your skin itch. On nights like that every booze
> party ends in a fight. Meek little wives feel the edge of the
> carving knife and study their husbands' necks. Anything
> can happen."

After several miles along Interstate 5 (another section of the El Camino Real and the final slash out of Pasadena) I merged onto State Route 133 heading south. Signs for its more telling and pleasant-sounding names – the

Laguna Freeway and Laguna Canyon Road – were a clear indication that I was on course for my latest chosen spot on the map. This welcome and winding two-lane led me through a peaceful valley in the San Joaquin Hills; thought to be the site of California's earliest recorded earthquake (1769). It was a far more natural setting of forested and chaparral-covered hillsides and small-town life (all noticeably settled along the northbound lane) that took me all the way back to the coast where the road leveled off, the hills receded and the town opened up to a view that came slowly into frame... the glistening blue Pacific at Laguna Beach.

Returning to the water always felt like a fresh start and a point of reference for wherever I was headed next. Like a terrestrial North Star of sorts guiding me down the coast. Each time one of the many back roads or mountain passes delivered me to that wide-open expanse, I welcomed the change of pace and scenery (just as when an extended shoreline drive returned me inland to roam among the trees). That recurrent back-and-forth between nature's blue and green kept this little outing new, colorful and engaging. Further, my fascination with ocean views never diminished – to the extent that each one typically began with several minutes of merely staring out across the water in contemplative silence. In *Blue Mind* Nichols writes a bit more eloquently that "the sea, once it casts its spell, does indeed hold us in its net of wonder forever."

A couple of fan palms swayed in the offshore breeze as I passed the iconic and picturesque Laguna Beach Lifeguard Tower at the water's edge where, once again, the air was noticeably cooler. It was another stretch of the PCH wisely left open and undeveloped as part of the city's "greenbelt" program. Of course, this was extremely appealing to me as I believe there is no better sight when arriving at the coast than an immediate view of the ocean (and no worse sight than, say... *no* sight of it).

Even though this affluent and artistic coastal town was just a waypoint in my travels, it seemed inviting enough to encourage a stop – not least for a late lunch and a review of my notes. Quickly finding my way to a little place just off the beach where much of the ambiance came courtesy of the sun, surf and sand, I chose a table under a large umbrella at the far end of the deck – suitably removed from the busier sections and perfect for some dedicated homework time. After settling in, ordering a drink and scanning the menu, I pulled out my journal – surely with the unquestionable resolve of a (*ahem*) serious writer – and immediately began staring out across the water.

Homework time… phooey.

ELEVEN
Bird of Passage

Every sunset brings the promise of a new dawn

~ Ralph Waldo Emerson

S topovers are a big part of the magic on road trips. Even when unplanned they tend to offer at least some measure of gratification – either along the way or upon arrival (often both). As with my nightfall change of lodging south to the harbor town of Crescent City, the remapping of my route from atop the Santa Cruz Mountains or that turnaround while deep in the bowers of Big Sur, the proverbial bumps in the road brought some unexpected wonders making them both easy and enjoyable to navigate. And my trek to Laguna Beach was no exception. What was merely a random point on the map chosen for little more than its location ended up ushering me through a silver lining of pleasant scenery and out to the commendable reward of a coastal setting. Any less-than-desirable stretches along the way were soon forgotten as I relaxed on that deck disregarding my journal for a time and remaining fully in the moment. And on the heels of that happy ending the next town I would stop in would be chosen with an equal amount of "care and consideration" – the simple allure of its name on a highway sign.

A long coastal run took me south past towns like Monarch Beach and Capistrano Beach on either side of the harbor city of Dana Point. A major port for trade ships in the early 1800s, it was described as "the only romantic spot on the coast" by its namesake and American lawyer and writer Richard Henry Dana, Jr. in his 1840 memoir *Two Years Before the Mast*. As the road beneath my wheels took on a low hum along this intermittently residential stretch, views both left and right were softened by flowering bushes and low-growth hardwood trees – planted as much for their aesthetic appeal as for their effectiveness as sound barriers. Though nothing to write home about (or, conversely, to send me into the ditch), this effort at camouflage was agreeable enough to keep me contentedly lost in song throughout the miles. And when those miles crossed into San Diego County just south of San Clemente, San Onofre Mountain gradually appeared to the east and I followed its foothills and folds to the town that enticed me simply with its telling name… Oceanside.

Although the palm trees of Southern California have long conjured up images of tropical climates and endless summers, a bit of research told me that most of those seen during my travels down the coast were imported. Bearing no fruit and standing too tall to provide any meaningful shade, they essentially had no inherent value. Originally planted by 18-century Spanish missionaries for practical and symbolic purposes, palms began to take on more of an aesthetic appeal in the early 20th century resulting in a massive beautification and planting effort all throughout Los Angeles.

As with the golden grasses so iconic to California and brought here by Europeans in the 1500s (both by chance in ship ballast and by design as food, medicine and ornamentation), early explorers were not met with many palm trees upon arrival – especially along the coast. But over time both have become anticipated and celebrated adornments; their images virtually synonymous with the state (some of the grasses now even known as "California annual type"). American historian Kevin Starr described this cultural ambition of enhancement and the palm tree's contribution to much of it in his 1985 book *Inventing the Dream: California through the Progressive Era:*

> "The sun was dramatically there, shining for more than 240 days a year, abundant of nurture and light… Southern California's turn-of-the-century conviction [was] that it was America's Mediterranean littoral, its Latin shore, sunny and palm-guarded."

As home to "King of the Missions" (Mission San Luis Rey de Francia - 1798), one of the longest wooden piers on the west coast (Oceanside Pier – 1888) and the California Surf Museum, Oceanside ("O'side" to locals) has an obvious allure that goes beyond that of its beaches. But for all these offerings and more it seems to be far better known for its abundance of that simple and exotic import… the palm tree. They were tall, evenly spaced and lining nearly every street I wandered along from the outskirts of town to the shoreline path known as The Strand. As the caw of seagulls carried on the breeze, a peaceful stroll on the wooden pier took me nearly two-thousand feet out over the water offering a wide-ranging view of this "palm-guarded" coast; the countless crowns and fronds easily visible against a brilliant sky. Indeed they were a visual highlight and an enticement to stay. And having spent the rest of my day at the water's edge in casual observation and relaxing in the sun, a comfortable weariness set in and Oceanside became my home for the night.

The peaceful and palm-guarded Strand at the water's edge

After a failed attempt to find even a modest oceanfront room, I checked into the aptly named Best Western Plus Oceanside Palms across from the harbor before taking a short walk into town and arriving at the Harbor House Café. As with The Flagship back in Pismo Beach, the nautically themed atmosphere was pleasant enough – even without a "Yacht Rock" soundtrack playing overhead. But there would be no fussing over notes this time; no deciphering my scribbling or researching any places of interest from the road. Just a casual meal, a rewarding drink and a little time to decompress by escaping into my Kindle where, as I greeted the *end* of my travel day, Muir (*Picturesque California*) "gladly welcomed the morning… and set forth in the exhilarating freshness of the new day…"

As for *my* new day… it brought with it a sneaking suspicion that it may be the last on this drive down the coast. Although keeping to my objective of not rushing through it; of simply meandering along the back roads in search of the long and scenic way 'round, the California-Mexico border was suddenly within reach. But there was a particularly unhurried feel about this morning. From a slightly later rise and unplanned "lobby" breakfast to an even more relaxed pace on the road, I wondered if I was subconsciously delaying the inevitable… or perhaps just savoring the remaining moments. Scanning the map before setting off, I made note of a few options along the "final mile" in an effort to get off the beaten path as soon as possible.

As the last of those Oceanside fan palms cast their long, mid-morning shadows across the Coast Highway, I continued south over the Buena Vista Lagoon (the only freshwater lagoon in California) for several slow and easy sun-streaked miles along the Pacific. Hugging the curve of this well-manicured section of coastline through the upscale town of La Jolla and crossing the byways and bridges of Mission Bay eventually led me to the peninsular town of Point Loma ("hill"). Originally settled as the fishing village of La Punta de la Loma de San Diego ("Hill Point of San Diego"), it's considered the landing place of the first European expedition – led by Portuguese navigator Juan Rodriguez Cabrillo (1542) – and, as I was pleased to discover, is often referred to as "the place where California began." This was a designation I couldn't resist – least of all for the unanticipated irony of (almost) ending my California drive where its history began. And so it was that during the planning stages of this trip Point Loma was immediately included as the last true stopover point.

A contrast of tree-lined residential neighborhoods and fenced-off military installations lined the way before a hilltop run through Fort Rosecrans National Cemetery (1882) offered views both far and wide. My windows down, I turned off the radio as a quiet sense of reverence and reflection seemed proper (and welcome). Passing neatly lined rows of brilliant white marble gravestones from military conflicts dating back to the 1800s while overlooking both the Pacific Ocean and San Diego Bay was as peaceful as it was moving. As final resting places go, it seemed ideal (and idyllic). A faint view of what I guessed was Tijuana, Mexico in the hazy distance of northern Baja California added to the surrounding sense of awe. Just beyond the cemetery a line of cars crept forward toward a small, gray gatehouse centered on the two-way road. The National Park Service arrowhead emblem (officially authorized in 1951) was posted on the facing wall; its features – a sequoia tree, a bison, mountains and water – familiar to me from travel books and other sightings along the coast. After paying my fee (and receiving confirmation that it was indeed Tijuana in the distance), I began wandering around the grounds of Cabrillo National Monument.

A casually descending run surrounded by coastal sage scrub and patchy remnants of the rare sea dahlia's large yellow blooms took me out to the New Point Loma Lighthouse (1891) at the southern tip of the cape. Situated behind tall palm trees and red-roofed Victorian cottages (the head keeper's residence), I later learned that the seventy-foot-tall pyramidal tower was manufactured in Trenton, New Jersey and is the only one of its kind on the west coast. The previous lighthouse (1855) was replaced when its perch of 422 feet above sea level – the highest of any lighthouse in the country – rendered it mostly ineffective; its light often obscured by fog and low-level clouds (at which time the keeper would have to fire a shotgun to warn ships away). But those were not the conditions on this day as nearby vista-point views of calm blue waters and rolling green hillsides persuaded me to stay and review some recently neglected notes. As makeshift work spaces go this, too, seemed ideal and it would be quite some time before I closed up shop to make my way over the hill to the park's namesake statue.

The second of two seven-ton, white stone effigies of Juan Rodriguez Cabrillo has been sitting atop this breezy, ten-mile-long peninsula overlooking San Diego and the distant San Ysidro Mountains since 1988. A gift from Portugal in 1939, the first sandstone statue was replaced when decades of exposure and vandalism took their toll. After a storied beginning with nearly as many twists and turns as Cabrillo's actual voyage, in 1949 it was placed near the original lighthouse before this more easily accessible spot became its permanent home in 1966. Panoramic views from the circular lookout point extended east across the resort town of Coronado ("crowned one") and the surrounding San Diego Bay where a few moored and drifting sailboats gave the impression of a tranquil painting. As with those back in Sausalito and Monterey, their hulls and mainsails brilliant splashes of white against a vast and deep-blue backdrop. A much hazier view along Mexico's Baja California coastline faded at the horizon and I wondered about some of the seaside villages and towns I had read about prior to setting out... Rosarito, Puerto Nuevo and Ensenada among others. But with no plan to cross the border (I was fewer than thirty miles from San Ysidro – one of the busiest border crossings in the world), it would be one of only a few distant views I wouldn't be visiting on this trip.

"The place where California began"

Following the arc of the harbor out of Point Loma and along Naval Base San Diego (principal homeport of the Pacific Fleet), I thought about my late father – a Navy veteran and musician who enjoyed traveling. As he had encouraged both this journey and its eventual telling on these pages, I quietly wondered if perhaps he was somewhere admiring all of it with me. When various signs began pointing out the obvious ("Cross Border Xpress"... "International Border - 3 Miles"), James Taylor's "Mexico" popped into my head and I realized I had been "radio silent" since my pass through Fort Rosecrans a few hours before. As so often occurs with any type of extended scenic outing – hiking, riding or driving – it's easy to get caught up in the moment without much deliberate awareness. And as those wistful lyrics played on a loop in my mind depicting Mexico as a laid-back paradise; I wondered if James was somehow trying to convince me of something... *"Woh, Mexico, it sounds so simple I just got to go, the sun's so hot I forgot to go home, guess I'll have to go now..."*

Just outside the small residential city of Imperial Beach at the southern tip of San Diego Bay lies an extremely rustic and tranquil area set hard against the Mexican border. The open spaces noticed earlier on the map led me to believe this would be a mostly desolate expanse – and indeed it includes some of the last undeveloped coastal wetlands in San Diego County. But the narrow and dusty road that ushered me into the Tijuana River Valley passed by several horse farms and riding stables as well as a seemingly endless run of fences as signs unsurprisingly warned of "Horse Crossing" and to "Yield to Horses." Miscellaneous trees offered little in the way of shade leaving the road occasionally cracked and crumbling; its shoulders caked in dry mud that kicked up as dust behind me. The namesake river running through this natural floodplain receives its water from creeks, streams and other small tributaries from the surrounding land – the majority of that in Mexico where wastewater and drainage issues have been a source of cross-border controversy for decades. And though foothills to the south appeared green and lush, much of the valley seemed ironically arid and fallow.

Following those foothills and fences west took me out to an apparently vacant Border Field State Park where the sage scrub flourished and one sign in particular made it clear just how close I was to Mexico: "Smuggling Is a Federal Felony." With the gates closed to vehicles on this day and me not being in hiking mode (nor footwear for the few-mile trek to the ocean), my later homework time would help round out the story of this quiet little corner of California where two countries meet seamlessly – at least in spirit.

A wildlife habitat to several endangered birds (the Western Snowy Plover and the California Least Tern among them), it's also home to International Friendship Park (1971) – a "binational park" atop Monument Mesa along the border at the water's edge where families and friends from both countries were once able to meet (and even embrace on Children's Day – a Mexican holiday). Although its noble purpose was to encourage international friendship while observing the end of the Mexican-American War (1848), the many restrictions now in place along the border have made that a far more challenging pursuit – the heavy steel mesh difficult even to see through. The pyramidal marble statue built to commemorate that time and truly serve as the "initial point of boundary between the United States and Mexico" originally straddled that boundary with a vertical dividing line at its base and an engraved dedication on each side – fittingly one in English and the other Spanish.

Long before much of the nearly 2000-mile border was so extensively sealed off, similar boundary monuments dotted the line from the Gulf of Mexico at the southern tip of Texas to the Pacific Ocean. But as settlements expanded in the late 1800s the original fifty-two markers grew to 258 and, in a sign of the times, the once-modest chain-link fence along this westernmost stretch became a massive steel structure (it, too, a source of cross-border controversy and extending 300 feet into the ocean). Today the fourteen-foot-tall marker (actually the first one constructed but officially designated "Monument Marker 258") sits just to the south in Mexico's Playas de Tijuana ("beaches of Tijuana") – the northwestern-most municipality in all of Latin America. This placement perhaps a nod to the park's intended purpose… and a goodwill gesture to our neighbors to the south.

While Imperial Beach is officially recognized as the "most southwesterly city in the continental United States" (along with its southernmost pier of the same name – 1909), this little patch of occupied land to the south – the Tijuana River Valley – can at least lay claim to being the most southwesterly *corner.* Although an offhand entry in my journal (and perhaps a modest designation to its residents), there was a very real sense of fullness that accompanied my visit here as it marked the close of this north-to-south, corner-to-corner and river-to-river (Smith to Tijuana) ramble down the coast. Trekking through big cities and small towns, along wide open beaches and winding back roads, into historic national parks, beneath ancient towering redwoods, over forested mountain passes, across scenic bridges of all types and, not least, through some hallowed musical and literary halls also carried with it some degree of accomplishment.

But it was a much greater feeling of gratitude that seemed to carry each day. As noted earlier my personal mantra of sorts was: *"Don't be surprised if things go wrong, but be grateful when they turn out well."* Whereas "the reward of a thing well done is to have done it" (Emerson), a drive down the coast is hardly a feat of any considerable effort or nobility. But after having spent each day as "a bird of passage generalizing on the immediate" (as Theroux so perfectly described it in *The Old Patagonian Express*), each moment of arriving safely was accompanied by a measure of appreciation and recognized quite simply for what it represented – and for all that we can truly hope for each morning... another good day.

Slowly making my way north along San Diego Bay toward the airport, I began to wonder when the last available flight home may be (10:45pm). There was certainly no plan or obligation to leave on this particular day and the notion of once more waking up in southernmost and sunny California to wander along a few more back roads was easily tempting. But as that sun began its initial dip toward the horizon I felt a sense of completion and contentment and I knew then that it was not only setting on the day – but on my journey as well. And as I drove those final miles reflecting on all the long and winding roads that brought me to that moment – roads which found me happily "between the wish and the thing" in search of, discovering and accepting wonders in all forms – one restless and consistent thought remained...

"What next?"

Conclusion

Do not then stumble at the end of the road

~ J.R.R. Tolkien

Travel is optimism in motion; an eagerness marked by hopeful anticipation, a sense of adventure and at least some measure of curiosity – likely the very reasons why so many are drawn to the roads less traveled. Those typically driven on only by locals… or that vanish among a canopy of trees… or meander for miles along a remote and rocky shoreline. And when the objective is to later take the reader along on the page, completely offering yourself to the experience and remaining present throughout is crucial. As American nature essayist John Burroughs once said: "The lure of the distant and the difficult is deceptive. The great opportunity is where you are."

It was with that outlook that I readily set off each morning to wander the many back roads and backdrops along the California coast – ultimately covering nearly three times as many miles as a direct run would have taken. To allow the journey to truly be the reward by passing slowly over the landscape, spending time in quiet contemplation at the water's edge or pausing to reconnect with an old friend and feeling a sense of home in the time shared.

Stopping every so often to smell the proverbial roses (and the literal grapes) gave me time to soak up my surroundings and eagerly anticipate what lay ahead. It also offered an intimacy that helped reframe any previously held images of this place with a fresh perspective. To see it again – in essence for the first time – and to let that experience inform my words. Words which at times were amusingly (perhaps even counterintuitively) spurred on by a favorite quote from the young protagonist Tom Joad in *The Grapes of Wrath* as he commented on his father's thoughts about writing:

> "Well, Pa wasn't no hand to write for pretty, or to write for writin'. He'd sign up his name as nice as anybody, an' lick his pencil. But Pa never did write no letters. He always says what he couldn' tell a fella with his mouth wasn't worth leanin' on no pencil about."

Rambling along the miles and allowing many of the "right" roads to be revealed to me on each outing heightened my awareness and offered a sense of freedom and adventure. Not knowing entirely (or in some cases at all) what path I would take next, which towns I would be stopping in or even where I'd spend the night were all welcome unknowns. As noted previously – a seemingly perfect way to experience the coast. Theroux commented on the appeal of this lack of restriction in *Deep South*:

> "I had become habituated to the spontaneity of my car, the ease of finding any open road, inserting myself into the life of the land by steering myself wherever I wished and stopping often. What I was doing was so different from

being an alien spectator on a train… the American South
had good roads…"

Each "road revelation" was an enjoyable opportunity for magic to
occur amid some of the more planned scenic, musical and literary stops.
And taking those unintended paths – where little discoveries were made
along the way – helped satisfy the curiosity that started this whole… *thing*.
And then it came time for leanin' on my pencil about it.

The simplest way for me to approach a project like this was to understand
that all it would take would be the ability to turn pages of notes (and a
phone full of pictures) into digestible stories. That – plus the unreserved
willingness to believe that in merely doing so all would turn out well. After
all it was *only* writing. And as Hemingway once stated so eloquently: "There
is nothing to writing. All you do is sit down at a typewriter and bleed."

As with the start of the trip itself, when I sat down at my "typewriter"
soon after returning I felt the immediate and quiet thrill of beginning
yet another journey – this one sure to be far more demanding, certainly
more time consuming and at times somewhat frustrating. A labor of love
undertaken with a level of enthusiasm and dedication matched only by
the eventual desire to be finished. As the protagonist Santiago said of his
fishing livelihood in Hemingway's *The Old Man and the Sea*: "It kills me
exactly as it keeps me alive."

So I pressed on; reviewing notes, scrolling through images and reliving
all the experiences in words until I eventually found myself contentedly
and somewhat wearily at the end of this road-and-written journey. Calling
to mind everything that brought me to this point; from the first mile to
the final word, offered a combined sense of meditation, satisfaction and
accomplishment and I felt grateful for the experience and that my goal –
however notable or modest – was realized.

In his 2016 anthology *Far and Wide: Bring That Horizon to Me!* Peart compared the end of his touring and recording career with Rush to his many travels by motorcycle. It was an apt analogy and a perfect summation of my thoughts – one I believe could serve equally well as a healthy outlook on life… *and* as the final word on this account of my drive down the coast:

> "That I could feel *good* about this occasion – well, I can only compare it to the way I feel at the end of a long motorcycle journey. I don't regret that the ride has to be over, but rather feel grateful for the miles I have traveled, for the sights along the way, and to be exactly where I am."

Acknowledgements

Thanks to everyone who wished me well on my ramble down the coast and who offered encouragement as I worked my way through this little writing project. I hope you enjoyed the drive as much as I did.

To Scot and Dorthy Ward for the kind invitation and gracious hospitality during my pass through town – *mi casa es tu casa*. To Harbor Master Charlie Helms for taking the time to clarify a few things about fog horns and maritime life as I explored the Crescent City waterfront. To Kara Sirianni for "finding" the keys to the other side of The Record Plant Sausalito and allowing me a private tour of that venerable and historic recording studio. To Steven Jesberg from the City of Capitola for his follow up about the Esplanade's decorative seawall. To Ashley Adams from the Los Angeles County Library for her kind and knowledgeable assistance about Topanga Canyon. To Ken Pfalzgraf from the Beverly Hills office of Urban Forest Management for answering my questions about some of the local flora. To Kathleen Tower for her image and graphics editing support. To artist Karl Moser whose talents brought my signage and snaking-road visions to life throughout. To my father for encouraging the drive and "eagerly looking forward" to this story about it. To my daughters Alea and Kelsey who always knew where to find me – tucked away in my office writing… *and writing… and writing*. And finally to Kell for seeing me off, for being that comfortable feeling of home whenever I checked in from the road and for bearing with me once again as I disappeared into my office immersed in this latest effort. *Te amo*.

The hardest part about writing a novel is finishing it
~ Ernest Hemingway

References

Bryson, Bill. *A Walk in the Woods - Rediscovering America on the Appalachian Trail*. New York, NY: Broadway Books, 1998.

Caillatt, Ken. *Making Rumours: The Inside Story of the Classic Fleetwood Mac Album*. Nashville, TN: Turner Publishing Company, 2012.

Chandler, Raymond. *Red Wind*. Cleveland, OH: World Publishing Company, 1946.

Collette, Doug. *Sympathy for the Drummer - Why Charlie Watts Matters*. Milwaukee, WI: Backbeat Books, 2019.

Crowe, Cameron. *The One and Only Peter Frampton*. San Francisco, CA: Rolling Stone Magazine, 1977.

Dana, Jr., Richard Henry. *Two Years Before the Mast*. Manhattan, NY: Harper & Brothers, 1840.

Doggett, Peter. *CSNY: Crosby, Stills, Nash and Young*. New York, NY: Simon & Schuster, 2019.

Ellison, Ralph. *Living with Music*. New York, NY: Random House, 2002.

Emerson, Ralph Waldo. *Nature*. Boston, MA: James Munroe and Company, 1836.

Felder, Don and Holden, Wendy. *Heaven and Hell: My Life in The Eagles (1974 - 2001)*. Hoboken, NJ: John Wiley & Sons, 2008.

Goldberg, Danny. *In Search of the Lost Chord: 1967 and the Hippie Idea*. Brooklyn, NY: Akashic Books, 2017.

Hemingway, Ernest. *The Old Man and the Sea*. New York, NY: Scribner, 1952.

Hemingway, Ernest. *The Sun Also Rises*. New York, NY: Simon & Schuster, 1926.

Jones, Tom. *Over the Top and Back: The Autobiography*. New York, NY: Blue Rider Press, 2015.

Kerouac, Jack. *On the Road*. New York, NY: Viking Press, 1957.

Mannes, Elena. *The Power of Music: Pioneering Studies in the New Science of Song*. New York, NY: Bloomsbury, 2011.

Muir, John. *My First Summer in the Sierra*. New York, NY: Houghton Mifflin, 1911.

Muir, John. *Picturesque California*. New York, NY: J. Dewing Publishing Company, 1888.

Muir, John. *The Mountains of California*. New York, NY: The Century Company, 1894.

Nichols, Wallace J. *Blue Mind: The Surprising Science That Shows How Being Near, In, On, or Under Water Can Make You Happier, Healthier, More Connected and Better at What You Do*. New York, NY: Little, Brown Spark, 2014.

Peart, Neil. *Far and Away: A Prize Every Time*. Chicago, IL: ECW Press, 2011.

Peart, Neil. *Far and Wide: Bring That Horizon to Me!*. Toronto, Ontario, Canada: ECW Press, 2016.

Peart, Neil. *Roadshow: Landscape with Drums - A Concert Tour by Motorcycle*. Cambridge, MA: Rounder, 2006.

Peart, Neil. *Traveling Music: The Soundtrack to My Life and Times*. Chicago, IL: ECW Press, 2004.

Schein, Richard. *Landscape and Race in the United States*. New York, NY: Taylor & Francis Group, 2006.

Springsteen, Bruce. *Born to Run*. New York, NY: Simon & Schuster, 2016.

Starr, Kevin. *Inventing the Dream: California through the Progressive Era*. Oxford, England: Oxford University Press, Inc., 1985.

Stegner, Wallace. *The American West as Living Space*. Ann Arbor, MI: Michigan Press, 1987.

Steinbeck, John. *Cannery Row*. New York, NY: The Viking Press, 1945.

Steinbeck, John. *East of Eden*. New York, NY: The Viking Press, 1952.

Steinbeck, John. *Journal of a Novel: The East of Eden Letters*. New York, NY: The Viking Press, 1969.

Steinbeck, John. *The Grapes of Wrath*. New York, NY: The Viking Press, 1939.

Steinbeck, John. *Travels with Charley - In Search of America*. New York, NY: Viking Press, 1962.

Theroux, Paul. *Deep South - Four Season on Back Roads*. New York, NY: Houghton Mifflin Harcourt, 2015.

Theroux, Paul. *Fresh Air Fiend - Travel Writings 1985-2000*. New York, NY: Houghton Mifflin Harcourt, 2000.

Van der Zwaag, M.D., *The Influence of Music and Mood and Performance While Driving*. US Nat'l Library of Medicine / Nat'l Institutes of Health, http://www.ncbi.nlm.nlh.gov/pubmed/22176481, 2012.

Soundtrack

Without You / 1973
Take It Easy / 1972
Crazy on You / 1975
Into the Mystic / 1970
Let Her Cry / 1994
Conga / 1985
City of New Orleans / 1972
Small Town / 1985
Solsbury Hill / 1977
What a Fool Believes / 1978
When the Levee Breaks / 1971
Do You Feel Like We Do / 1976
Dreams / 1977
Hollywood Nights / 1978
Time Stand Still / 1987
American Girl / 1976
Get Together / 1967
The Camera Eye / 1981
San Francisco (Be Sure to Wear Flowers in Your Hair) / 1967
Knocking at Your Back Door / 1984
Windsong / 1975
Rocky Mountain High / 1972
Heart of Gold / 1972
One Particular Harbor / 1983

Ventura Highway / 1972
Roadhouse Blues / 1970
Long Cool Woman (In a Black Dress) / 1971
(Get Your Kicks) On Route 66 / 1946
All I Wanna Do / 1993
Hotel California / 1976
For What it's Worth (Stop, Hey What's That Sound) / 1966
Sunset Grill / 1984
Babylon Sisters / 1980
Mexico / 1975

Lightning Source UK Ltd.
·Milton Keynes UK
UKHW011841011220
374466UK00009B/594/J

9 781665 506373